Forth LITE
Tutorial

Leo Wong

Juergen Pintaske

Stephen Pelc

July 2014/July2018

1 Charles Moore - Forth - The Early Years: Background information about the beginnings of this Computer Language

2 Charles Moore - Programming A Problem Oriented Language: Forth - how the internals work - **Now as eBook and as print book**

3 Leo Brodie - Starting Forth, the classic

4 Leo Wong / Juergen Pintaske / Stephen Pelc FORTH LITE TUTORIAL: Code tested with MPE VFX Forth, SwiftForth and Gforth

5 Juergen Pintaske – A START WITH FORTH – Article Collection – 12 Words to start, then 35 Words, Javascript Forth, much more

6 Stephen Pelc - Programming Forth: Version July 2016

7 Tim Hentlass - Real Time Forth

8 Brad Rodriguez - Moving Forth / TTL CPU / B.Y.O. Assembler

9 Chen-Hanson Ting - Footsteps In An Empty Valley issue 3

10 Chen-Hanson Ting - Zen and the Forth Language: EFORTH for the MSP430G2552 from Texas Instruments

11 Chen-Hanson Ting - eForth and Zen - 3rd Edition 2017: with 32-bit 86eForth v5.2 for Visual Studio 2015

12 Chen-Hanson Ting - eForth Overview

13 Chen-Hanson Ting - FIG-Forth Manual and Test on FPGA 1802

14 Chen-Hanson Ting - EP32 RISC Processor IP: Description and Implementation into FPGA – ASIC tested by NASA

15 Chen-Hanson Ting – Irriducible Complexity

16 Burkhard Kainka - Learning Programming with MyCo: Learning Programming easily – PC independent (Forth code to follow soon)

17 Burkhard Kainka - BBC Micro:bit: Tests Tricks Secrets Code, Additional MicroBit information, running the Mecrisp Package

18 Burkhard Kainka&Thomas Baum – Sparrow Programs, TINY13

Contents

Print version v6a July 2018

Introduction

When I started looking for an Entry Level Tutorial for Forth for my own learning, the one found http://www.murphywong.net/hello/simple.htm seemed to be most suitable for me.

I contacted Leo, and he allowed me to use his basic version as a starting point to go through the fun of learning Forth myself a bit more and while I tried it out, I added all the answers plus some more, so you can see what exactly has to appear on the screen when running the Forth code.

There is the usual issue with tutorials: entry level, mid range or high level? I tried here the entry level – for me. Digestible for people who want to start with Forth.

With more background knowledge you will read through it more quickly. Some smaller parts might be too difficult to understand – just skip them.

And a link to more advanced tutorials: http://www.forth.org/tutorials.html

You can try out the examples shown here yourself by downloading the compiler from www.MPEFORTH.com.

And there is anoother book as part of the Forth Bookshelf that is available now A START WITH FORTH.

Working through this tutorial, I had 2 windows open: one on the left side of my PC with the eBook and next to it the window of the Forth compiler; it worked very well for me with copy and paste, and I hope you will enjoy it as well. This would all be running on the PC: eBook reader and MPE Forth compiler. You might have to download a Kindle eBook reader but it is free. See http://www.amazon.com/gp/feature.html?docId=1000493771

There might be issues with different PC or Mac versions, in such a case you might have to type in the examples yourself rather than copy and paste.

I had started this as print book first, before I wanted to convert to eBook. As I have no control over character size for example when you read it as eBook, I tried to find ways to make it readable, sorry, if it does not look as neat and formatted anymore in some places.

Thanks to Leo for letting me take over and to Stephen at MPE Forth for his support.

In the meantime, MPE has published an Embedded Forth version running completely on the microcontroller, the PC is only used as terminal; one version for the ARM and one for the MSP430 Launchpad, I have added some information at the end here, or see the extensions done later in A START WITH FORTH..

This sequel of this tutorial will continue from here and use real hardware, e.g. the TI Launchpad.

Any feedback please to epldfpga@aol.com.

I will try to add additional information onto www.exemark.com as time allows.

Or have a look at www.Forth-ev.de – the German Forth group.

This Tutorial is the third eBook on Forth published in this sequence. Our current list of eBooks was at the time

Forth – The Early Years goo.gl/y2Zlud

Forth – Programming a Problem Oriented Language goo.gl/SVRdyF

MyCo Starting Programming for Beginners
– and the code ported to Forth soon goo.gl/vnuivT
Not much Forth code in there yet, but things are planned in the background already.

The classic book to look at as well is Starting Forth by Leo Brodie, see it as PDF at
http://www.exemark.com/FORTH/StartingFORTHfromForthWebsitev9_2013_12_24.pdf

or as part of the Forth Bookshelf,

or on the Forth Inc. website. Some examples in this book might not be compatible with the VFX Forth used here. We have not tried them but it is definitely a very good read.

Thanks to all of the people who helped me to make this tutorial happen.

First of all Leo, then Stephen from MPE, Dirk Bruehl and Mike Kalus, and the many others that gave inputs.

Patrick my son and Barbara my wife have to be mentioned as well, they helped with the design, corrections and checking.

Ground 0 - *What is* Forth and what is Forth LITE*?*

Forth is, among other things, a programming language whose ideals are freedom and simplicity. Freedom requires much knowledge and responsibility, and simplicity is yet more demanding.

"LITE" here means the basic part of the language. *Forth* LITE attempts to teach the basics of Forth. It is a very powerful programming language, and seeing all of the features might frighten you. In Forth you use a layered approach. You start with the minimum and expand to more complex levels as needed. This is not much different to learning to speak a new language: you learn a minimum set, good enough to communicate and expand your knowledge as needed.

How to try the examples in this tutorial
Let's look at Forth in general first. Forth is inherently interactive. Programming in Forth is carried out rather like a dialog between you and a machine that understands Forth. You send the machine some code by typing it in, the carriage return ends your input, so the Forth knows it has to react now. Depending on the circumstances, the machine responds by trying either to perform ("execute") what you typed in or to put this information into memory and remember ("compile") the code.

If the machine then says something like "ok", that's good. If it doesn't say ok, it might still be ok. Try sending more code until the machine explicitly objects (or pretends to be dead).

A machine that knows Forth is: a Forth Machine. Sometimes I don't distinguish between Forth and the machine.

1. Start up a <u>Forth system</u>, and type in the examples (The link takes you to more Forth information). Most Forths accept source from your hard drive, but you'll get a better feeling for Forth by entering into a give-and-take with the computer. Where you see a space, press the spacebar. At the end of a line, press the key on your keyboard that means "Enter".

2. If the machine doesn't understand something you entered it may respond by repeating what it didn't understand and adding an error message or maybe just: ?. Check to see if you typed in the example correctly. If not, type it in again.

3. In Forth named procedures to be executed are called words. Some frequently used words are very short. For example, the word . displays a signed (plus/minus) integer. In general, what is punctuation in other languages are procedures in Forth.

4. Many Forths are case sensitive. All the examples will work in uppercase. If you try lowercase and the machine says ok, use whatever case you wish.

Now from the general Forth that exists in many flavours to VFX Forth, the one used in this tutorial. If you try it out as two windows on the screen: one for the eBook and one for VFX Forth, remember that one window is active (blue bar on top) only, and the other window is inactive (grey bar on top). You can only type into the blue window, as I had to find out myself though I should have known.

In a written book I can space text out quite nicely as it would not change after print. But unfortunately data is displayed differently with eBooks, and this changes depending on the device you read it on.

I have defined the following convention:
What you have to input is the first line, you end the input with the CR/Enter key.
\\ defines what the Forth computer will answer
\ defines additional comments added for you
As \ means to Forth ignore all characters until the end of the line, the next CR, so \\ means the same to Forth.

Start up a Forth and try:
\ do not forget to hit the RETURN / ENTER key, whatever it is called on your computer

Type in

1 .   and hit Return/Enter to tell your PC to work on it
```
\\ 1
\ puts 1 onto the stack, then . moves this information
down from the stack and displays it on the screen
```

Forth always reads from left to right,
and from now on we will not put the CR at the end of the input, you will know by now to hit the Enter/Return button on your keyboard and will do it automatically:

```
1 . 2 . 3 .
\\ 1 2 3
\ 3 values are stored onto the stack, then back down
and printed on to screen
```

Spaces are separators between the data and the Forth word to execute:

```
12 . 3 . 123 .
\Try it out yourself.
```

Your machine probably won't understand this:

aieee!
\\ error undefined word
\ you tried to tell Forth to do something it cannot understand

.

\\ data stack underflow
\ the stack is empty, so there is a stack error message

So in this first lesson we already learned 3 Forth words:

A space separates data and commands/words in Forth, at least one space is needed.

\ tells Forth to ignore what follows until the next CR.

. grabs data from the stack and displays it.

It should be understood when it's time to go or you are tired:

BYE

\ shuts VFX Forth down, you have to start it again to continue your tutorial, so you might not use BYE and continue

IMPORTANT: the VFX free download version has some restrictions as you know. One of them is the fact that new words created in a session are NOT added permanently to the dictionary. You will lose them if you type BYE in your VFX.

Lesson 1 - *The Forth Programmer's Interface*

According to Leo Brodie's book *Thinking Forth*, the three characteristics of the Forth Programmer Interface are:
implicit calls, you call an activity,
implicit data passing, you pass data to an activity,
and direct access to memory, you manipulate data in memory.

None of these characteristics is unique to Forth, but they form quite a combination.

The following examples use Forth words that will be explained later.
For now, just type each line exactly as you see it and observe how your Forth responds.

1. Implicit calls. The word .S is called by entering its name, .S.

Try:

```
.S
\\ DATA STACK    empty stack
\ show all of the data that is on the stack now; as we
have not entered anything yet, the stack is empty
```

2. Implicit data passing. The word 1+ takes a number and returns another without specifying either. The word DROP takes a number without returning one.

Try:

```
.S
\ answer see above, display what is on the stack, but
leave it there

7
\\
\ save 7 onto the stack

.S
\\   7
\ display what is on the stack

1+
\\
\ add 1 to the number on the stack

.S
\\   8
\ display the new number top of stack
```

1+
****
\ add another 1 to the top of stack

.S
**** 9
\ display the top of stack

DROP
****   \ DROP the top value on the stack

.S
**** DATA STACK empty stack
\ now the stack is empty again as the 9 has been
dropped / removed

3. Direct access to memory.
In Forth you can name addresses of memory and see and change the data
at those addresses.

An address of memory identifies an "address unit".
The size of an address unit is often 8 bits - too small to hold a number
greater than 255.
Forth typically works with "cells". The size of a cell is usually two, four, or
more address units. Numbers considerably larger than 255 fit comfortably
in a cell.

To name a memory address MINE, *and reserve the cell of memory at*
MINE *try:*

CREATE MINE   1 CELLS ALLOT
\ create 1 memory address, call it MINE

To put a number in this cell of memory at address MINE *try:*

1 MINE !
\ 1 belongs to address MINE, and store this 1 at
location MINE

To see the contents of the address units in the cell of memory at MINE *try:*

MINE 1 CELLS DUMP
**** 004C:94A0   01 00 00 00 04 64 75 6D 70 73 00 00 00 00 00 00
.....dumps
****

To display the number in the cell of memory at MINE *try:*

MINE ?
**** 1
\ just displaying this cell, not a block as above

To change the number in this cell of memory at MINE *try:*

1024 MINE !
\ 1024 is the value MINE has to take !

MINE 1 CELLS DUMP
\\ 04C:94A0   00 04 00 00 04 64 75 6D   70 73 00 00 00 00
00 00 .....dumps

MINE ?
\\ 1024
\ showing the 1024, rather than the hex 04 00

-1 MINE !
\ set to -1

MINE 1 CELLS DUMP
   \\ 004C:94A0   FF FF FF FF 04 64 75 6D
   \\   70 73 00 00 00 00 00 00   .....dumps

MINE ?
\\ -1
\ as expected -1

<u>**BYE**</u>

Lesson 2 - *Forth in One Sentence*

And the sentence is: "Forth is a programming language that uses two stacks and a predefined dictionary of words that a programmer adds to in writing a program."
```
\ and the last word defines thus, how you call the
application - in both meanings
```
Words, dictionary, two stacks: the essence of Forth.

In lesson 1 I wrote, that the Forth programmer interface is characterized by implicit calls, implicit data passing, and direct access to data. All three of them we have done in lesson1

Calls are implicit, because when a Forth sees a text with a space before and after, it thinks "word" and tries to find it in its dictionary. If it finds it, it will immediately do something with it.
If Forth doesn't find it in its dictionary, it will then try to understand it as a number; if that fails, Forth will confess its failure and send a failure message.

Data passing is implicit because Forth words get their input from the data stack and return their output to the same data stack.

Access to data is direct because the addresses of the data are recorded in the dictionary.

Lesson 3 discusses the Forth data stack.
Lesson 4 discusses the Forth dictionary.
Addresses will have to wait until Lesson 21

BYE

Lesson 3 - *"The Stack"*

Words in this lesson: .S   DROP

All Forths have at least two stacks. The stacks work similarly but serve different purposes.

A stack is a way of managing data. With a stack, data is added to and taken from the "top", as with a stack of dishes. The acronym for this is LIFO: Last In First Out. The top of the stack is called TOS (Top Of Stack). If there's no TOS, the stack is empty. A stack is such a convenient way of managing data that most (all?) programming languages use it internally.

The stack discussed in this lesson is the Forth DATA STACK: Forth programmers call it "the stack". The second Forth stack, called the RETURN STACK, will be discussed later. Some Forth implementations have additional special-purpose stacks for floating-point numbers or for strings. These special stacks hold data that it may be convenient to keep separate from the data on "the stack".

Words take and return numbers from the stack. When you type in a number, its destination is the stack. The following examples use the words .S and DROP. .S displays the numbers on the stack in stack order, TOS (top of stack) on the right. In some Forths, .S also tells you how many numbers are on the stack.
DROP removes the TOS item, reducing the number of items on the stack by one.

Try:

```
.S \\DATA STACK empty stack
\ here we have an empty stack
```

```
10
\ now add 10 to the stack
```

10 is now TOS:

```
.S
\\   10 0000:000A
\ shown as 10   and hexadecimal A
```

Now try:

```
20
\ 10 is still there as before and the 20 is put on top
of it on the stack
```

20 is now TOS, and 10 is below 20:

.S
```
\\ 20 0000:0014  10 0000:000A ok-2
\ 20 on top, 10 below, all ok, 2 values on the stack
```

Now try:

DROP
```
\\ ok-1
\ one value, the 20 is dropped, 10 left on the stack
```

The word DROP *removed 20 from the stack. TOS is again 10:*

.S
```
\\ 10 0000:000A  ok-1
\ 10 on stack, hex value is A, all ok, 1 value (10) on
the stack
```

Now try:

DROP
```
\\   ok
\   nothing to display as nothing on the stack, so just
all ok
```

The word DROP *removed 10 from the stack. The stack is now empty:*

.S
```
\\ DATA STACK empty stack
\ and the stack is empty again
```

BYE

Lesson 4 - *The Dictionary*

Words in this lesson: WORDS SEE

About all a Forth system knows is contained in its dictionary. The dictionary contains words - words the system came with, and words defined by the programmer. By "word" is meant: the word's name, which Forth uses to look up the word, and the word's action, which is code that Forth either executes or compiles.

The dictionary comes with the Forth system. The programmer writes a program by adding to the dictionary words defined in terms of words in the dictionary.

As a rule, Forth finds a word by starting with the most recently defined word and working backwards. If two or more words in the dictionary have the same name, Forth will use the most recently defined and be satisfied. Re-use of names is allowed but probably isn't *Forth LITE*.

Most Forths have the words WORDS and SEE. WORDS displays the names of all words currently in the dictionary. A "fat" Forth will have lots a words - the names will whizz by unless the display pauses. A "thin" Forth will have far fewer - the names might fit onto a single screen. SEE followed by a word's name tries to display the word's definition. SEE may or may not display definitions of words defined in assembly language.
There is no harm in seeing what Forth can SEE.

You basically drill down deeper and deeper into the dictionary, more for the specialist.
Non-specialists just look or skip it.

Try:

WORDS
```
\ WORDS will show all of the WORDS this Forth has, for
VFX many hundred, this is why Forth LITE starts with a
reduced number
```

SEE WORDS
```
\\ WORDS   ( 00414B8C E893FFFFFF )   CALL 00414B24 WORDS
( 00414B91 C3 ) NEXT,   \\ ( 6 bytes, 2 instructions )
ok
\ shows what the word WORDS consists of
```

SEE SEE
```
\\ SEE     ( 0044FF64 E8D3FFFFFF )   CALL 0044FF3C DIS
( 0044FF69 C3 ) NEXT, ( 6 bytes, 2 instructions )  ok
\ shows what the word SEE is made up of
```

```
SEE .S     \  see the result in the appendix, too long
for here
SEE ?
\\ ?       ( 00414A80    8B1B )     MOV EBX, 0 [EBX]   (
00414A82    E8AD77FFFF ) CALL     0040C234  . (
00414A87    C3 )  NEXT,  ( 8 bytes, 3 instructions )
ok
\ the same for the word ?
SEE !
\\ !
\\  ( 0040A8B0    8B5500 ) MOV       EDX, [EBP]
\\  ( 0040A8B3    8913 )   MOV       0 [EBX], EDX
\\  ( 0040A8B5    8B5D04 ) MOV       EBX, [EBP+04]
\\  ( 0040A8B8    8D6D08 ) LEA       EBP, [EBP+08]
\\  ( 0040A8BB    C3 )                NEXT,
\\  ( 12 bytes, 5 instructions )  ok
\ shows the maschine code the word ! executes
               \
```

Now let us define our first own Forth word.
: starts the definition of a new word
; finishes it
SPACE, and at least one, is the separator between Forth words

```
: HELLO   ." Hi! " ;
\\ ok
\ : starts a new word
\ Hello is the name of this word
\ ," means what follows now is to stay as ASCII and is
probably to be printed / displayed
\ " tells Forth, here is the end of this string of
characters
\ ; ends the definition of the new word
\ and do not forget the CR so Forth knows it has to
start working on it
```

Now let us execute our first word, we just type it in, followed by CR:

```
HELLO
\ prints Hi! To the terminal
\ and for the specialists:
\ SEE HELLO
\\ ( 004C94C0    E81335F4FF ) CALL  0040C9D8    (.")
"Hi! " ( 004C94CC    C3 ) NEXT,  ( 13 bytes, 2
instructions )  ok
```

It was so easy, let us define a second word:

```
: GOODBYE  ." Bye! " ;
\ define the new word GOODBYE, if called to print Bye!
```

to the terminal
\ otherwise exactly the same as Hello

GOODBYE
\ print Bye!

And for the specialists:

SEE GOODBYE
\\ GOODBYE (004C94F0 E8E334F4FF) CALL 0040C9D8 (.")
"Bye! " (004C94FC   C3)   NEXT, (13 bytes, 2 instructions
)

And it is easy to combine the functions of existing words:

: **QUICK**   **HELLO GOODBYE** ;
\ define a new word QUICK using the ones defined before

QUICK
\\ Hi! Bye!
\ prints both

So you get a first feeling how you program in Forth

And for the specialist again:

SEE QUICK
```
\\ QUICK
\\ ( 004C9520     E89BFFFFFF )
\\ CALL          004C94C0          HELLO
\\ ( 004C9525     E8C6FFFFFF ) CALL
\\    004C94F0        GOODBYE    ,
\\ ( 004C952A     C3 )                   NEXT,
\\ ( 11 bytes, 3 instructions )
```

BYE

Lesson 5 - *Adding to the Dictionary*

Words in this lesson: :   ;   \

By far the most common way of adding a word to the dictionary is to write a colon definition. Some colon definitions we have written in lesson 4 already, they start with the Forth word : and end with the Forth word ; .
After : comes the name, then the definitions, then ; .

This is a commonly cited Forth definition:

```
: SQUARED   DUP * ;
\ use 3 spaces rather than just one after the new word
definition and 1 space to separate words for better
visibility
```

Forth reads from left to right. The definition of SQUARED tells Forth:
when you see the word SQUARED,
first do DUP – duplicate the value on top of the stack, so two values now,
then do * - multiply the values top of stack and top of stack – 1 and leave the result on top of the stack.
In addition the two values have been removed.

As in Forth data is passed implicitly via the stack, it is considered bad practice to define a word without documenting what data (if any) it takes from the stack and what data (if any) it returns to the stack.

The canonical way of doing this, is to use the Forth word (- left bracket which tells the system to ignore what follows up to and including the next) - right bracket.
Expectations ("before") and results ("after") are separated by --.
The resulting (before -- after) is a "stack-effect comment".

So:

```
: SQUARED   ( n -- n*n )  DUP * ;
\ take value n on top of the stack, and replace it n*n
```

It's also wise to document what the new word does and add an explanation. For this the Forth word \ back slash is useful. \ tells Forth to ignore the rest of the line.

So try:

```
\ Return square of n
: SQUARED   ( n -- n*n )  DUP * ;
```

```
\ Skip next line if your system doesn't SEE the word
SEE SQUARED
```

2 SQUARED

```
.S
\\   DATA STACK    top    4 0000:0004    ok-1
```

SQUARED

```
.S
\\   DATA STACK    top   16 0000:0010    ok-1
```

SQUARED

```
.S              \\   DATA STACK    top 256 0000:0100   ok-1    #
```

DROP
```
\ result 256 is dropped from the stack and the stack is
empty again
```

For extra credit read:

Leo Brodie's <u>Forth Style Guide</u>
This is not the most recent document but will add to your understanding and shows how to pronounce some of the somehow cryptic word definitions. And do not forget, you can always define a new word and give it a name that you understand better – definitely helpful in the beginning.

For example

```
: Stack_dis_rem . ;
\ display one stack entry and remove it
```

```
: NDSD .S ;
\ non destructive stack display of all stack entries
```

And you might want to have a look at Paul Bennett's <u>Forth Coding Rules</u>. I expect there will be a reformatted version of this on the ExMark website soon for download and print if you wish. A standard way of coding and documenting will help others to go through your code more easily. And this will probably be the same for you if you look at your code a year later.

<u>BYE</u>

Lesson 6 - *Forth Arithmetic Part 1*

Words in this lesson: + - * /

Most words don't wait before acting. So the stack has to be prepared well
as most data will be taken from there in general. The word + doesn't ask
"plus what?"; it removes the top two stack numbers and returns their sum to
the top of the stack.
The words - * / also take the top two stack numbers and return a result.

Try:

```
1 1 +

.S
\\  DATA STACK  top  2 0000:0002  ok-1
\ there is one value on stack now and it is 2

1 +

.S
\\  DATA STACK  top  3 0000:0003  ok-1    \
\ 2 was on stack, so 1 added to it


1 1 +
\\  ok-2  \
\ old number 3 and new entry 1 + 1 = 2 on stack

.S
\\  DATA STACK  top  2 0000:0002  3 0000:0003  ok-2
        \ both 3 and 2 on stack

+
\ add  the 2 values on stack  3+2 = 5

.S
\\  DATA STACK  top  5 0000:0005  ok-1
\ one value on stack now 5

DROP
\ remove this 5 from the stack
```

– *subtracts TOS from the number below it.*

*You are not sure about the sequence which number subtracted from which
one? I remember it with 10-1=9 gives 10 1 -, so the TOP is subtracted from
the number below.*

Try them all in sequence to see the stack behaviour:

1 1 -
\\ ok-1
\ put one onto the stack, put another 1 on and subtract
from first one below TOS top of stack

.S
\\ DATA STACK top 0 0000:0000   ok-1
\ 1 - 1 = 0 left on the stack

1 -
\\ ok-1
\ subtract one from the value on the stack which is
here 0

.S
\\ DATA STACK top -1 FFFF:FFFF   ok-1
\ -1 (FFFF:FFFF) on stack now

1 1 -
\\ ok-2
\ put 0 onto the stack, this is now TOS,
\ -1 is on stack below from before

.S
\\ top 0 0000:0000   -1 FFFF:FFFF   ok-2
\ the 2 values 0 and -1 on stack
\ remember: .S displays first TOS and then the ones
below

-
\\ ok-1
\ calculates 0 - 1 = -1, leaves -1 on stack

.S
\\ DATA STACK   top -1 FFFF:FFFF   ok-1

DROP
\\ ok
\ drop TOS = -1 from the stack, so stack is empty now

* multiplies the top two stack numbers. Try:*

2 2 *

.S
\\ DATA STACK   top 4 0000:0004

2 *

.S
\\ DATA STACK top   8 0000:0008

2 2 *

```
.S
\\ DATA STACK top   4 0000:0004   8 0000:0008   ok-2
\ new 4 on top of old 8

*

.S
\\ DATA STACK top  32 0000:0020   ok-1
```

DROP
```
\  and clear the stack
```

/ *takes the number below TOS and divides it by TOS.*

Try:

100 2 /
```
.S
\\ DATA STACK top  50 0000:0032   ok-1   \
\ result is 50 in decimal and 32 in hexadecimal
```

2 /
```
.S
\\ DATA STACK top  25 0000:0019   ok-1   \
```

2 /
```
.S
\\ DATA STACK top  12 0000:000C   ok-1   \
\ 12, but no remainder 0.5 here, rounded down
\ we will come back to this later
```

4 2 /
```
.S
\\ DATA STACK top  2 0000:0001   12 0000:000C   ok-1 \
```

```
/
\ divide

.S
\\ DATA STACK top  6 0000:0006 \
```

DROP
```
\ empty stack, discard the 6
```

Forth reads from left to right. There is no "operator precedence." Try:

```
\ 1 + (2 * 3)
\ UUUPS a window Windows Exception
\  Interception shows up on my PC, not allowed

2 3 * 1 +
\ This is the correct way to enter it in Forth
```

```
.S
\\ DATA STACK top     7 0000:0007   ok-1
```

DROP

1 2 3 * +   \ 1 2 3 on stack, 2*3=6 on stack, 1 + 6 = 7

To make it clearer: numbers are added to the stack as you enter them.

So 1 2 3
When Forth sees the word * – immediate action
So 1 2 3 * changes into 1 6
When Forth sees the word +, the the two top values are added and the result put back, here a 7.

```
 .S
\\ DATA STACK top     7 0000:0007   ok-1    \
```

DROP   \ empty stack

```
.S
\\ DATA STACK empty stack    ok \
```

1 2 + 5 *
\ 1 onto stack, 2 onto stack, add 1+2=3 and 3 back onto stack, 3*5=15 and 15 back on stack

```
.S
\\ DATA STACK top    15 0000:000F
```

DROP
\ empty stack

There's a lot to observe in these examples.
You might want to repeat them with different numbers before saying:

<u>**BYE**</u>

Lesson 7 *Forth Arithmetic Part 2*

Words in this lesson: /MOD   MOD   */MOD   .

In lesson 6 you saw that 100 2 / 2 / 2 / left 12 on the stack. The
words + - * / are all integer operators. / gives the quotient of n1 divided
by n2.

But the remainder is not lost,
use either /MOD, which returns the quotient as TOS and the remainder
below TOS,
or MOD, which just returns the reminder.

Here are the stack effects of + - * /MOD / MOD:

```
+      ( n1 n2 -- n1+n2 )
\ leaves the sum, only one value

-      ( n1 n2 -- n1-n2 )
\ leaves the difference, only one value

*      ( n1 n2 -- n1*n2 )

\ leaves the multiplication result, only one value

/      ( n1 n2 -- quotient )
\ leaves just quotient on stack, remainder lost

MOD  ( n1 n2 -- remainder )
\ leaves just the remainder on stack

/MOD ( n1 n2 -- remainder quotient )
\ leaves quotient as TOS and the remainder below TOS

*/MOD ( n1 n2 n3 -- remainder quotient )
\ leaves quotient as TOS and remainder below TOS
\ as you multiply first, larger number
\ before divide, better resolution

.      ( n -- )
\ displays the signed integer n on top of the stack
\ removes it from the stack,
\ not like .S with displays
\ but leaves the stack untouched
```

Try:

1 .
\ put 1 on stack, display and remove

-1 .
\ put -1 on stack, display and remove

7 -1 + .
\ 7 onto stack, -1 onto stack as TOS, add display 6 and remove 6 from the stack

10 10 /MOD . .
\\   1   0   ok-2
\   10 / 10 = 1 remainder 0

10 11 /MOD . .
\\   0 10   ok-2
\ 10/11 leaves a number smaller than 1, the integer of this is 0
\ so the remainder is the 10 we started with

10 3 /MOD . .
\\   3   1   ok-2
\ 10/3=3 and leaves a remainder of 1 as shown above

10 3 / .
\\   3   ok

\ here just the integer number 3 and no remainder

10 3 MOD .
\\   1 ok

\ the same division, but looking only for the remainder

10 3 /MOD 3 * + .
\\ 10   ok
10 onto the stack, 3 onto the stack
\ /MOD, 10/3=3 (TOS), remainder 1 underneath
\ 3 onto stack, so now 3 3 1;
\ *, so 3*3=9, 9 back onto the stack, so now 9 1
\ + 9+1=10
\ . display 10 and remove from stack

5 10 20 */MOD
\\ top   2 0000:0002   10 0000:000A   ok-2 \
\ 5 10 20 onto the stack
\ */MOD, take the first 2 and multiply 5*10=50
\ now divide 50/20 = 2 and remainder 10

.S
\\ DATA STACK top   2   0000 0002   10   0000 000A ok-2

The result is TOS, so you can continue with your calculations. The remainder is underneath, so you might use it later or DROP it.

BYE

Lesson 8 *Forth Arithmetic Part 3*

Words in this lesson: 1+ 1- ABS   NEGATE MAX   MIN */

Here are some other arithmetic words to try.

Take one, leave one:

1+ (n -- n+1)
\ Faster execution than 1 + otherwise the same effect,
like increment number on stack

1- (n -- n-1)
\ Faster execution than 1 - otherwise the same effect,
like decrement number

ABS (n -- u)
\ Return absolute value of n, e.g. 5 is 5 absolute and
-5 is 5 as absolute number

NEGATE   (+n|-n -- -n|+n)
\ Return the arithmetic inverse of n, so 100 changes to
-100,

Take two, leave one:

MAX (n1 n2 -- n1|n2   \ Return the greater of
                             \ n1 and n2

2 9 MAX
\\ ok-1

\ easy to understand here, but 2 and 9
\ might be variables, where the value is not known
.S
\\ DATA STACK   top 9 0000:0009 ok-1

MIN (n1 n2 -- n1|n2)
\ Return the lesser of n1 and n2

2 9 MIN
\\ok-1
\ the smaller number of 2 and 9 should be on stack
.S
\\ DATA STACK   top   2 0000:0002   ok-1
\ as expected

Take three, leave one:

```
*/   ( n1 n2 n3 -- quotient )
\ Same as n1 n2 * n3 / but faster
```

Take three, leave two:

```
*/MOD   ( n1 n2 n3 -- rem quot )
\ Same as n1 n2 * n3 /MOD
```

For */ and */MOD, avoid overflow during the multiplication process, and the quotient must be within the range of signed integers.
As example the temperature measurement conversion:

```
\ Celsius <-> Fahrenheit conversion
\ °F =  °C * 1.8000 + 32.00
\ °C = ( °F -   32 ) /1.8000
: C  ( Celsius -- Fahrenheit )  9 5 */  32 + . ;

100 C
\\  212  ok

0 C
\\ 32  ok

: F  ( Fahrenheit -- Celsius )  32 -  5 9 */ . ;
\ °C = (°F -  32.00)/ 1.800

212 F
\\ 100  ok

32 F .
\\ 0  ok


BYE
```

Lesson 9 - *Managing the Stack 1*

Words in this lesson: DEPTH

.S, as discussed in lesson 3, displays all the numbers on the stack. DEPTH
(-- +n) returns how many of those numbers they are.
"Number" can stand for various things:

signed integer,
unsigned integer,
address,
count,
ASCII code,
UNICODE,
true/false flag,
etc,

So we will for now refer to stack *items*. All the *items* on the stack are the
same size: one *cell*.
The size of a *cell* depends on the Forth implementation.
A cell must be at least 16-bits; nowadays 32-bits is probably the most
common. How many bits there are in a cell determines, how much
information a cell can hold - more about this in a later lesson.

So in somewhat technical terms, the word DEPTH (-- +n) returns as
TOS the number of one-celled items that were on the stack BEFORE
DEPTH was called.

Note that the stack-effect comment doesn't indicate these items, because
DEPTH doesn't require that there are any items on the stack and doesn't
affect the items that may be on the stack, except of course, to push them
one item deeper in the stack by making +n TOS.

DEPTH
\\ DEPTH ok-1

The word DEPTH has counted the number of items on stack and added
this number to the stack. This is why now we have 1 item on stack

.s

\\ DATA STACK top 0 0000:0000 ok-1

And with some data on stack

20 30 44
\\ ok-3
\ load 3 items on the stack

```
.S
\\ DATA STACK
\\ top
\\   44 0000:002C
\\   30 0000:001E
\\   20 0000:0014
\\ ok-3
```

DEPTH
```
\\ ok-4
\ so the 3 stack items and the DEPTH value on stack now
```

```
.S
\\ DATA STACK
\\ top
\\    3 0000:0003
\\   44 0000:002C
\\   30 0000:001E
\\   20 0000:0014
\\ ok-4
```

Define a new word, to check and display how many items are on stack and remove the DEPTH item, so the stack is unchanged.

```
\ Tell how many items are on the stack
:  DEPTH?  ( -- )  DEPTH . ;
\ define DEPTH? to take the value DEPTH,
\ display it and discard it from the stack
```

DEPTH?
```
\\ 0  ok
```

10
```
\ put an item onto the stack
```

DEPTH?
```
\\ 1  ok-1
```

20
```
\ add 20 to the stack
```

DEPTH?
```
\\ 2  ok-2
```

30
```
\ add 30 to the stack
```

DEPTH?
```
\\ 3  ok-3
```

```
.S
\\  DATA STACK
\\ top
```

```
\\   30 0000:001E
\\   20 0000:0014
\\   10 0000:000A
\\ ok-3
```

.

```
\\ 30  ok-2
\ remove one item
```

DEPTH?
```
\\   2  ok-2
```

.

```
\\   20  ok-1
\ display and remove another one
```

DEPTH?
```
\\   1  ok-1
```

.

```
\\   10  ok
```

```
\ and the last one
```

DEPTH?
```
\\            0  ok
```

Some Forths empty the stack when they encounter a word not in the dictionary; others don't. To find out what your Forth does, try:

10 20 30

DEPTH?
```
\\ 3  ok-3
```

Now input an undefined word:

Nonce
```
\\ Err# -13 ERR: Undefined word.   -> nonce
```

DEPTH?
```
\\ 0  ok
\ so VFX clears the stack,
\ as 10 20 30 have disappeared
```

BYE

Lesson 10 - *Managing the Stack 2*

Words in this lesson: DUP   ?DUP   OVER   SWAP   ROT
PICK   ROLL   NIP TUCK 2DROP 2DUP 2OVER 2SWAP

Some people do not like the fact that items and words have to be entered in the right processing sequence as there are no brackets.

But the fact that items on the stack sometimes have to be shifted around is even more difficult for them to imagine. But it is basically the same point as before: get it in the right sequence before processing, so it is part of the planning before implementing it.

The big advantage of calculating via the stack: you do not need addresses where your data is, they are predefined and wait in the right sequence (or are manipulated). No addresses needed and data stored in memory cannot unintentionally be overwritten.

Let's assume we have 4 numbers that we have to use and we have no stack:
One way is to define locations/places and put them there, e.g. on your desk:
(1) 22 top left
(2) 45 bottom left
(3) 68 top right
(4) 94 bottom right
You reserve this space for them and memorize where they are with memory location (e.g. top left) and contents (22).
You can use this method in Forth as well, but you use the Stack as much as possible.

In Forth you will try to store them on the stack in the right sequence if possible for later processing, or do a bit of stack processing where needed. No memory addresses needed at all.

With something as strict as a stack (LIFO = Last In First Out), some stack management might be necessary, to re-order the data as it came in, to a sequence on the stack needed for the next calculations. Forth provides the words for it.

For example, if you want a copy of TOS (Top Of Stack) as you need it 2 times, you DUPlicate it. We used this already to multiply a number with itself.

If you want a copy of the item below TOS and put it on top of TOS, you bring it OVER.

If you want TOS and the item below it to switch positions, SWAP them.
If you want the third stack item to be TOS, you ROTate it to the top.

```
DUP    ( x -- x x )
\ Copy TOS xx 11     -- 11 11

?DUP   ( x|0 -- x x | 0 )
\ Copy TOS if it isn't zero     xx 11   -- 11 11

OVER   ( x1 x2 -- x1 x2 x1 )
\ Copy x1 to TOS
\ xx 11 22 -- 11 22 11

SWAP   ( x1 x2 -- x2 x1 )
\ Switch positions x1 and x2,
\ xx 11 22 -- 22 11

ROT    ( x1 x2 x3 -- x2 x3 x1 )
\ Rotate x1 to TOS,
\ 11 22 33 -- 22 33 11
```

As you probably know by now, all of the words in your Forth are used to
define new words. These words above could be (but likely aren't) defined in
terms of the words PICK and ROLL:

```
PICK   ( xu ... x0 u -- xu ... x0 xu )
\ Copy xu to TOS
\ 11 22 33 44 55   (3) -- 11 21 31 41 55 33

ROLL   ( xu ... x0 u -- xu-1 ... x0 xu )
\ Rotate xu to TOS
\ 11 22 33 44 55   (5) -- 22 33 44 55 11

: DUP  ( x -- x x )  0 PICK ;
\ 1   -- 1 1

: OVER  ( x1 x2 -- x1 x2 x1 ) 1 PICK ;
\ 1 2    -- 1 2 1

: SWAP  ( x1 x2 -- x2 x1 )  1 ROLL ;
\ 1 2    -- 2 1

: ROT  ( x1 x2 x3 -- x2 x3 x1 ) 2 ROLL ;
\ 1 2 3    -- 2 3 1
```

Forth programmers generally don't use PICK and ROLL if avoidable, and
prefer specific to general solutions.
In this way you avoid the temptation to treat the stack as an array.

On the other hand, these definitions wouldn't be unusual:

```
\ Drop the second stack item, the one below TOS

: NIP  ( x1 x2 -- x2 ) SWAP DROP ;
```

```
: /  ( n1 n2 -- quotient )    /MOD NIP ;
```

```
: MOD  ( n1 n2 -- remainder ) /MOD DROP ;
```

NIP and TUCK are probably CODEd in assembly language, but one could define for example:

```
\ Copy TOS below the second stack item
: TUCK  ( x1 x2 -- x2 x1 x2 )  SWAP OVER ;
```

The words that concern pairs of stack elements are probably also in assembly language to be faster and not made up of Forth words:

```
\ Drop top two stack items
: 2DROP  ( x1 x2 -- )  DROP DROP ;
```

```
\ Duplicate top two stack items
: 2DUP  ( x1 x2 -- x1 x2 x1 x2 )  OVER OVER ;
```

```
\ Copy lower pair over top pair
: 2OVER  ( x1 x2 x3 x4  -- x1 x2 x3 x4 x1 x2)
   3 PICK  3 PICK ;
```

```
\ Exchange top two cell pairs
: 2SWAP  ( x1 x2 x3 x4 -- x3 x4 x1 x2 )
   3 ROLL  3 ROLL ;
```

Managing the stack well comes with experience. Now look at this this:

```
\ Math Family - try to write down, how the stack values
are shifted around

\ ." and CR in this definition to be discussed later

: "+"  ." + " ;
\ define the word "+" to display +

: "-"  ." - " ;
\ define the word "-" to display -

: "="  ." = " ;
\ define the word "=" to display =

: FAM  ( n1 n2 -- )
   2DUP +
   DUP 2OVER          CR . "+" . "=" .
   DUP 2OVER SWAP     CR . "+" . "=" .
```

```
    DUP 2OVER SWAP ROT   CR .  "-" .  "=" .
                         CR .  "-" .  "=" .  ;
```

6 6 FAM
```
\\ 6 + 6 = 12
\\ 6 + 6 = 12
\\12 - 6 = 6
\\12 - 6 = 6   ok
```

4 2 FAM
```
\\ 2 + 4 = 6
\\ 4 + 2 = 6
\\ 6 - 4 = 2
\\ 6 - 2 = 4   ok
```

Did somebody say we need 3DUP as well? Let's define it

: 3DUP (x y z -- x y z x y z)
   2 PICK 2 PICK 2 PICK ;

4 7 9 3DUP
```
\\ ok-6
```

.S

```
\\ DATA STACK
\\  top
\\   9 0000:0009
\\   7 0000:0007
\\   4 0000:0004
\\   9 0000:0009
\\   7 0000:0007
\\   4 0000:0004
\\  ok-6
```

Homework: redefine FAM using 3DUP.

To imagine how items move on stack using these words is difficult in the beginning. It helped me a lot to do it by hand:

In the appendix you will find a table of the words. Do a screen print, cut them out and try the stack movements.

Or write them onto sticky notes.
Lego bricks are another option, write the words you want to use on the side or a bit of sticky tape. Then you can stack them and see do the stack manipulation.
Here in this tutorial we mainly look at their name and what happens when they are used.

It will become a lot easier, when you start writing small Forth programs and suddenly have to modify the sequence of items on the stack.

BYE

Lesson 11 - *Programming by Teaching and Learning*

You program in Forth by teaching a machine new actions that you and the machine know by name. Each new action is a novel arrangement of known actions, perhaps mixing in some data.

By being added to the dictionary, this new action can be used to teach still newer actions. You choose the names, so a good part of the communication between you and machine is in your terms.

The machine knows a lot of Forth, probably more than you do – but is has well and rigidly defined ways of doing things. It will make it easier for you if you teach it well and add meaning to the newly defined word.

As you saw, among the Forth words the machine knows, are DUP and *. You might therefore teach it:

```
: SQUARED  ( n -- n**2 )  DUP * ;
\ duplicate item on stack and multiply

: CUBED  ( n -- n**3 )  DUP SQUARED * ;
\ duplicate the value, do SQUARED and then * again

: 4TH  ( n -- n**4 )  SQUARED SQUARED ;
\ Do SQUARED times SQUARED
```

…and so on until you have taught it all the words your program needs to do.

Forth is inherently interactive in comparison to many other languages. You add to your program in small bits and test them immediately.

Bugs are found early in the design cycle as you do a constant program/compile/test.

With Forth you can teach the machine whatever a computer can do. As you teach you learn, because any word you add to the dictionary you can (and should) immediately test.

A few more words:

```
\ ." displays text, needs " to end the text

: ME  ( -- )  ." Leonardo DiCaprio" ;
\\ ok
\  The new word ME
```

ME
\\ Leonardo DiCaprio ok
\ Oops!

Redefine ME

: **ME** (--) ." **Tutorial User**" ;
\\ ME is redefined ok
\ this word ME replaces the old ME,
\ both are still in dictionary

Let's test if both are there:

ME
\\ Tutorial User ok

FORGET ME
\\ ok
\ this deletes the latest me from the directory

So, is the older ME still there?

ME
\\ Leonardo DiCaprio ok
\ yes, the older ME is still there

BYE

Lesson 12 - *Thoroughly Modern Forth*

In lesson 9 I talked about stack items, the size of a cell, noting that an item could represent different kinds of data:
a signed integer,
an unsigned integer,
an ASCII code (character),
a true/false (or Boolean) flag,
etc.

It used to be in earlier Forths that a cell was 16-bit wide, period.
Then came 32-bit processors and 32-bit Forths, and now there are 64-bit and 128-bit processors. The notion is that in every Forth a stack item (and by implication some other kinds of data) is the size of a cell, but that the size of a cell is determined by the implementation, and allows for easier porting of Forth programs between different kinds of computers.

The number of bits (binary digits) in a cell determines how many different bit patterns the cell can distinguish, which determines how many different values of a particular kind of data a cell can accommodate.

For instance, one bit can distinguish two different patterns: 0 1, which could be interpreted as:
the unsigned integers 0 and 1
the signed integers 0 and -1 or (maybe) -0
the Boolean flags false and true
etc.

Two bits can distinguish four patterns: 00 01 10 11, which could be interpreted as:
the unsigned integers 0 1 2 3
the signed integers 0 1 -2 -1
the Boolean flags false(=00) and true(<>false)
etc.

We can generalize and say that n-bits can distinguish $2^{**}n$ (2 to the power of n) different patterns.

Getting down to cases:,
a 16-bit cell can distinguish 65,536 different patterns, each of which could represent:

An unsigned integer between 0 and 65,535
a signed integer between -32,768 and 32,767
the Boolean flags false(=0000000000000000) and true(<>false)
etc.

A 32-bit cell can distinguish 4 294 967 296 patterns, each of which could represent:

An unsigned integer between 0 and 4,294,967,295
a signed integer between -2,147,483,648 and 2,147,483,647
the Boolean flags false(=00000000000000000000000000000000) and
true(<>false)
etc.

Try the following:

```
-1 U.
\\ 4294967295  ok
```

If 65535 is displayed, your Forth has 16-bit cells.
If 4294967295 as with VFX, then there are 32-bit cells.
If another number is displayed, then either the size of cell is other than 16 or 32 bits, or your Forth represents numbers atypically.

Forth easily handles data bigger and smaller than the size of one cell:
"double" (2-cell) numbers and
"floating-point" numbers,
"bits",
"characters",
"strings" of ASCII characters,
database fields and records,
files,
"objects",
etc.

But for now we still stay with one kind of data - cell-sized signed integers.

BYE

Lesson 13 – *Comparisons*

Words in this lesson: TRUE   FALSE   =   <   >   0=
0<

Comparisons are important, as the result will be a flag – TRUE or FALSE – and based on the value of this flag, you take decisions what to do next.

A flag tells you for instance, whether TOS is equal to the stack item beneath TOS. Your Forth may already have the words TRUE and FALSE, which return to TOS "well formed" true and false flags.

A well-formed true flag has all bits set (1), while a well-formed false flag as all bits "reset" (0). It is highly likely that in your Forth all bits set has the same bit pattern as the integer -1 and all bits reset has the same pattern as the integer 0.

So TRUE is any value except 0
and FALSE is defined by 0.
Easy to remember: any number is TRUE, and
0 / nothing / not TRUE so FALSE

Try:

```
TRUE  .
\\  ok-1

.S
\\ DATA STACK
\\  top
\\    -1 FFFF:FFFF
\\  ok-1

FALSE  .
\\  ok-2

.S
\\ DATA STACK
\\  top
\\    0 0000:0000
\\   -1 FFFF:FFFF
\\  ok-2
\ 0 for FALSE as TOS and below -1
\ or all bits set for TRUE
```

If your Forth doesn't have TRUE *or* FALSE *you can teach it easily:*

CONSTANT defines a new word that always returns the same value

```
0 CONSTANT FALSE
```

```
FALSE .
\ = returns a true flag if the top two stack items
\ are equal
```

```
FALSE FALSE = CONSTANT TRUE
```

```
TRUE .
```

or

```
1 Constant True
\\ TRUE is redefined  ok-4
\\ true  ok-5
```

```
.S
\\ DATA STACK
\\  top
\\    1 0000:0001
\\   -1 FFFF:FFFF
\\    0 0000:0000
\\    0 0000:0000
\\   -1 FFFF:FFFF
\\  ok-5
```

and

```
. . . . . .
\\ 1 -1 0 0 -1 ok
\ as one possibility to clear the stack
```

Each of these comparison words returns a well-formed flag as TOS:

```
=    ( n1 n2 -- flag )
\ Does n1 equal n2 ?
```

```
1 2 =
\\  ok-1
```

```
.S
\\ DATA STACK
\\  top
\\    0 0000:0000
\\  ok-1
\ here 0, so not equal
```

```
>    ( n1 n2 -- flag )
\ Is n1 greater than n2 ?
```

```
1 2 >
\\  ok-2
```

```
.S
\\ DATA STACK
```

```
\\  top
\\   0 0000:0000
\\   0 0000:0000
\\ ok-2
```

< (n1 n2 -- flag)
\ Is n1 less than n2 ?

1 2 <
```
\\ ok-3
```

.s
```
\\ DATA STACK
\\  top
\\  -1 FFFF:FFFF
\\   0 0000:0000
\\   0 0000:0000
\\ ok-3
\ yes
```

0= (n -- flag)
\ Does n equal 0 ?

And so on

0< (n -- flag)
\ Is n less than 0 ?

Try these examples:

1 2 + 2 1 + = .
```
\\   -1  ok
\ yes they are equal, 1 2 +  = 3,  2 1 + = 3,  3 = 3
```

.s
```
\\ DATA STACK
\\  top
\\  -1 FFFF:FFFF
\\ ok-1
```

1 2 - 2 1 - = .
```
\\   0  ok
\ no, not equal  1 2 - = -1, 2 1 - = 1  -1 not equal 1
```

3 4 * 4 3 * < .
```
\\   0  ok
\ no   12 is not greater than 12
```

3 4 / 4 3 / < .
```
\\   -1  ok
\ yes 3/4  is smaller than 4/3
```

```
5 6 /  6 5 / > .
\\    0  ok
\ no  5/6   is NOT greater than 6/5

5 6 MOD  6 5 MOD > .
\\-1  ok
\ yes, 5 6 mod (remainder = 5)
\ is greater than 6 5 mod (remainder =1)

1 -1 + 0= .
\\-1  ok
\ yes  1 + (-1) = 1 - 1 = 0 equals    0=

1 -1 - 0= .
\\ 0  ok
\ no   1 - (-1) = 1 + 1 = 2   not equal 0=

-1  0< .
\\-1  ok
\ yes  -1 is 0< smaller or equal to 0

-1 -1 * 0< .
\\ 0  ok
\ no  (-1) * (-1) = +1 and not smaller or equal to 0
```

Given these comparison words, others are easy to define. Your Forth may already have them, try it before you define them new:

```
\ Does n1 not equal n2 ?
: <> ( n1 n2 -- flag )  = 0= ;
\ not equal to

\ Does n not equal 0 ?
: 0<> ( n -- flag)  0= 0= ;
\ not equal to 0
\ Frequently seen synonym for 0=

: NOT  ( n -- flag ) 0= ;


\ Is n1 greater than or equal to n2 ?
: >= ( n1 n2 -- flag ) < NOT ;
\ Is n1 less than or equal to n2 ?

: <=  ( n1 n2 -- flag ) > NOT ;
```

BYE

Lesson 14 - *Conditional Execution*

Words in this lesson: IF ELSE THEN

Executing either of two blocks of code, depending on the flag on stack. This is how to tell Forth to execute words conditionally:

```
flag not 0:  IF   do-this                        THEN

flag is  0:  IF              ELSE   do-that THEN
```

or in words:

IF (flag on stack is 1, so yes) do this, and then jump over ELSE to THEN

IF (flag on stack is 0, so no) jump over words to ELSE, execute the code there and continue with THEN

With loop defined as
        IF xxx xxx xxx   ELSE yyy yyy yyy yyy   THEN

The execution will be

Flag 0   IF ELSE yyy yyy yyy yyy   THEN
\ jump to else execute code

Flag 1   IF xxx xxx xxx   THEN
\ execute, then jump to THEN

Use IF ELSE THEN only within colon definitions (this means between : and ;). IF and THEN must be within the same definition.
ELSE is optional as there might be no code executed, but if used, ELSE must come between IF and THEN.
This describes only this construct, words can come before IF and others to follow THEN.

Try writing two inefficient but understandable definitions:

```
: EVEN? ( n -- )  2 MOD IF ." odd" ELSE ." even" THEN ;
\ define the word EVEN?, puts 2 on the stack
\ then divide the entered number to be tested by 2
\ we are only interested in the remainder
\ if dividable by 2 there will be no remainder,
\ 0 on stack
\ this as flag means 0 so FALSE,
\ so when IS tests, jump to ELSE
\  and send even to the screen
\ if remainder not 0, flag means TRUE for IF
\  and odd is sent.
```

1 EVEN?
\\ odd ok
\ no this is an odd number

2 EVEN?
\\ even ok
\ yes, this an even number
\ Careful, the stack effect of IF is (flag --),
\ so if this flag as TOS is needed after the test
\ make a copy with DUP before the test
\ as the flag is taken off the stack by IF.

: ABS (n -- +n) DUP 0< IF -1 * THEN ;
\\ ABS is redefined ok-1

1 ABS .
\\ 1 ok
\ as positive already, no change

-1 ABS .
\\ 1 ok
\ absolute value of -1 is   1

IF ELSE THEN *can be "nested". Try:*

: SCORE (n --)

DUP 89 > IF ." Honors"
\ duplicate the number entered as needed later
\ is this number larger than 89, so 90 or more
\ if flag is 1 type "Honors"

ELSE DUP 69 > IF ." Pass"
\ 89 or smaller then, duplicate the number entered
\ is it more than 69, so 70 to 89 if 1 print "Pass"

ELSE ." Fail"
\ else print "Fail", number between 0 and 69

THEN
\ go back one nested level

THEN DROP ;
\ finish the first IF, DROP the number entered

100 SCORE
\\ Honors ok
\ more than 89 is HONORS 89 is PASS

80 SCORE
\\ Pass ok
\ 80 is PASS as more than 69

```
60 SCORE
\\ Fail ok
\  69 and lower gives FAIL
```

In Forth the true flag need not be "well formed" - have all bits set.
Any flag with at least one bit set is taken to be true. Try:

```
0 CONSTANT FALSE
\ define 0 as the constant FALSE
```

```
FALSE 0= CONSTANT TRUE
\ if FALSE is not 0 then the
\ resulting constant is TRUE
```

```
: TRUE?  ( n -- )

  DUP TRUE = IF  ." Well-formed true"  ELSE

  DUP        IF  ." Still true"        ELSE

                 ." False"

              THEN THEN  DROP ;
```

```
TRUE TRUE?
\\ Well-formed true ok  \
```

```
FALSE TRUE?
\\ False ok             \
```

```
-1 TRUE?
\\ Well-formed true ok  \
```

```
1 TRUE?
\\ Still true ok        \
```

```
2 TRUE?
\\ Still true ok        \
```

```
0 TRUE?
\\ False ok             \  0 is FALSE flag
```

Well, I hope this was not too confusing.

BYE

Lesson 15 - *Repeated Execution*

Words in this lesson: EXIT   BEGIN   AGAIN   UNTIL WHILE   REPEAT

Much of the computer's power comes from its ability to do something repeatedly and fast.
The easy way to tell Forth to do something again is to just to repeat the word or phrase:

Try:

```
\ Add five numbers
: SUM5   ( n1 n2 n3 n4 n5 -- sum ) + + + + ;

14 26 33 25 18 SUM5 .
\\ 116  ok   \\
\  put the 5 numbers onto the stack,
\  execute SUM5,
\  display TOS
```

Repeating words or phrases is quite legitimate but limiting. If you have to repeat it 10 or more times, there must be other ways.

In this lesson we will show three other ways of repeating execution ("looping").
Each of them begins with the word BEGIN :

BEGIN ... AGAIN
```
\ this is an endless loop
```

BEGIN ... UNTIL
```
\ in this loop the end condition is on the stack
```

BEGIN ... WHILE ... REPEAT

BEGIN AGAIN UNTIL WHILE REPEAT, like IF ELSE THEN, are used in colon definitions, with BEGIN and AGAIN, BEGIN and UNTIL or BEGIN ... WHILE ... REPEAT in the same definition (in Forth, other "control structures" can be developed, but we'll just use these for now).

I will soon use these words in three definitions of a word named INTEGERS.

But first another word that is also used only in colon definitions: EXIT.
EXIT just says: stop executing the word I'm in.

Try:

```
\ Display 1 2 3
: JUST3  ( -- ) 1 . 2 . 3 . EXIT 4 . 5 . ;
```

```
JUST3
\\  1 2 3  ok  \
```

EXIT *just affects the word it's in. Try:*

```
\ Display 1 2 3 4 5
: TO5  ( -- )  JUST3  4 . 5 . ;
```

```
TO5
\\ 1 2 3 4 5  ok
\  TO5 will execute JUST3, type 1 2 3, then EXIT,
\ then execute the rest 4 . 5 .
```

We will need the word EXIT because in our first definition of INTEGERS, the words between BEGIN ... AGAIN will repeat unconditionally.

Try:

```
\ Display integers 1 ... +n using BEGIN ... AGAIN
: INTEGERS  ( +n -- )

  1 BEGIN  2DUP < IF 2DROP EXIT THEN  DUP . 1+  AGAIN ;
  \ 1 onto stack, begin the loop,
  \ duplicate the top 2 numbers on stack
  \ if smaller drop 2 top items on stack and exit,
  \ else duplicate top item, print, add 1
  \ and again
  \ EXIT happens when number entered
  \ and number incremented from 1 are equal
```

Remember to have EXIT in such a loop.

```
10 INTEGERS
\\  1 2 3 4 5 6 7 8 9 10  ok   \
```

```
1 INTEGERS
\\  1  ok                      \
```

```
0 INTEGERS
\\  ok
\ 0 integers are displayed
```

BEGIN ... AGAIN executes the words between BEGIN and AGAIN *again and again* unless Forth executes EXIT, which in INTEGERS happens when +n is less than TOS.

Many published Forth definitions are very short - one or two lines.
The best way to understand them (and to go about defining your own
words) is to write them out one word or phrase to a line along with stack
and other comments.

Here is the definition of INTEGERS one word to a line, explaining the action
of each word and the resulting stack activity:

```
: INTEGERS    ( +n -- )
    1
\ Initialize i to 1
 ( +n i=1 )
      BEGIN
\ Start loop: i is TOS
( +n i )
      2DUP
\ Duplicate 2 items
( +n i +n i )
      <
\ Is +n less than i ?
( +n i flag )
      IF
\ Act on flag
( +n i )
          2DROP
\ True: drop 2 items
(   )
          EXIT
\ True: leave word
(   )
      THEN
\ End IF ... THEN
(   )
      DUP
\ DUPlicate TOS
( +n i i )
      .
\ Display TOS
( +n i )
      1+
\ Increment TOS
( +n i=i+1 )
    AGAIN
\ Loop back
( +n i )
    ;
\ End definition
```

Word, description and stack activity would be better in one line, but I wanted to avoid any eBook issues.

You might see the above example correctly on your reader as formatted:

```
: INTEGERS   ( +n -- )
   1              \ Initialize i to 1     ( +n i=1 )
   BEGIN          \ Start loop: i is TOS  ( +n i )
      2DUP        \ Duplicate 2 items     ( +n i +n i )
      <           \ Is +n less than i ?   ( +n i flag )
      IF          \ Act on flag           ( +n i )
         2DROP    \ True: drop 2 items    ( )
         EXIT     \ True: leave word      ( )
      THEN        \ End IF ... THEN       ( )
      DUP         \ DUPlicate TOS         ( +n i i )
      .           \ Display TOS           ( +n i )
      1+          \ Increment TOS         ( +n i=i+1 )
   AGAIN          \ Loop back             ( +n i )
   ;              \ End definition
```

```
10 INTEGERS
\\  1 2 3 4 5 6 7 8 9 10  ok  \
```

```
1 INTEGERS
\\  1  ok                        \
```

```
0 INTEGERS          \
\\  ok                           \
```

BEGIN ... UNTIL repeats execution *until* there's a true=1 flag just before UNTIL.
The words between BEGIN and UNTIL execute at least once, since UNTIL tests whether to leave the loop.

Like with the IF construct, UNTIL swallows the flag, and as with IF, a true flag need not be "well formed". Here's the second definition of INTEGERS:

Try:

```
\ Display integers 1 ... +n using BEGIN ... UNTIL
: INTEGERS   ( +n -- )
   1 BEGIN  2DUP < 0= IF DUP . THEN 1+ 2DUP < UNTIL
2DROP ;
\\  ok  \
```

```
10 INTEGERS
\\ 1 2 3 4 5 6 7 8 9 10  ok \
```

```
1 INTEGERS
\\ 1  ok                      \
```

```
0 INTEGERS
\\ ok                         \
```

Here is the second definition one word to a line:

```
: INTEGERS ( +n -- )
  1
\ Initialize i to 1 ( +n i=1 )

  BEGIN
\ Start loop: i is TOS
( +n i )

    2DUP
\ Duplicate 2 items
( +n i +n i )

    < 0=
\ Is +n NOT less than i ?
( +n i )

  IF
\ Yes?
( +n i flag )

    DUP
\ Duplicate i
( +n i i )

      .
\ Display i
( + n i )

  THEN
     1+
\ Increment TOS
( +n i=i+1 )

      2DUP
\ Duplicate 2 items
( +n i +n i )

     <
\ Is +n less than i ?
( +n i flag )

  UNTIL
\ Loop back unless true
( +n i )
    2DROP
\ Drop two items
( )
;
\ End definition
\\  ok  \
```

```
14 INTEGERS
\\   1 2 3 4 5 6 7 8 9 10 11 12 13 14   ok   \
1 INTEGERS
\\   1   ok                                       \
0 INTEGERS
\\   ok                                               \
```

The BEGIN ... WHILE ... REPEAT construct executes the words between BEGIN and WHILE,
continues execution to REPEAT *while* there's a true flag just before WHILE,
then at REPEAT loops back to the word just after BEGIN.

If the flag just before WHILE is false, execution skips to after REPEAT.
The words between BEGIN and WHILE will execute at least once. If the flag before WHILE is false the first time through, the words between WHILE and REPEAT will not execute at all.

WHILE, like UNTIL, swallows its flag, which need not be well formed. So if needed again later DUP it.

```
BEGIN xxx xxx xxx (wf)WHILE yyy yyy yyy (rf)REPEAT
```

Four options now:

wf=0 rf=0
```
BEGIN xxx xxx xxx (wf)WHILE yyy yyy yyy (rf)REPEAT
```
\ skip WHILE block, jump over REPEAT

wf=0 rf=1
```
BEGIN xxx xxx xxx (wf)WHILE yyy yyy yyy (rf)REPEAT
```
\ skip over while block, back to xxx

wf=1 rf=0
```
BEGIN xxx xxx xxx (wf)WHILE yyy yyy yyy (rf)REPEAT
```
\ continue to WHILE block, jump over REPEAT

wf=1 rf=1
```
BEGIN xxx xxx xxx (wf)WHILE yyy yyy yyy (rf)REPEAT
```
\ continue through WHILE block and back to xxx

Here's the third definition:

Try:

```
\ Display integers 1 to +n using BEGIN  WHILE  REPEAT
: INTEGERS  ( +n -- )
   1 BEGIN  2DUP < 0= IF  DUP .  1+  REPEAT  2DROP ;
```

```
10 INTEGERS
\\ 1 2 3 4 5 6 7 8 9 10   ok      \

1 INTEGERS
\\ 1   ok                         \

0 INTEGERS
\\ ok                        \
```

The third definition with line comments:

```
: INTEGERS   ( +n -- )
   1
\ Initialize i to 1
( +n i=1 )

   BEGIN
\ Start loop: i is TOS
( +n i )

      2DUP
\ Duplicate 2 items
( +n i +n i )

      < 0=
\ Is +n not less than i ?
( +n i flag )

   WHILE
\ If true, continue else
\ jump to after REPEAT
( +n i )

      DUP
\ DUPlicate TOS
( +n i i )        .
\ Display TOS
( +n i )

      1+
\ Increment TOS
( +n i=i+1 )

   REPEAT
\ Loop back
( +n i )

   2DROP
\ Drop two items
(  )

   ;
\ End definition
```

15 INTEGERS
\\   1 2 3 4 5 6 7 8 9 10 11 12 13 14 15   ok   \

2 INTEGERS
\\   1 2 ok   \

0 INTEGERS
\\   ok   \

<u>**BYE**</u>

Lesson 16 - *Counted Loops*

Words in this lesson: ?DO DO I J LEAVE UNLOOP LOOP +LOOP

Forth understands several kinds of *counted loops*,
in which stack arguments before the loop determine the number of
iterations.

I recommend that you just use for now:

+n 0 ?DO ... LOOP

which executes the words between ?DO and LOOP exactly *+n* times and not
at all if *+n* equals zero.

Like BEGIN, etc. ?DO, etc. should only be used in colon definitions.

Try:
```
: INTEGERS  ( +n -- )
  1 SWAP  0 ?DO  DUP .  1+  LOOP  DROP ;

10 INTEGERS
\\ 1 2 3 4 5 6 7 8 9 10   ok   \

1 INTEGERS
\\ 1   ok                       \

0 INTEGERS    \\ ok                          \
```

With line comments, here I just left it as a block, hopefully you see it
correctly:

```
: INTEGERS  ( +n -- )
    1         \ Initialize i          ( +n i=1 )
    SWAP      \ Set limit for ?DO     ( i limit=+n )
    0         \ Set index for ?DO     ( i limit index=0 )
    ?DO       \ Start counted loop    ( i )
       DUP    \ DUPlicate i           ( i i )
       .      \ Display i             ( i )
       1+     \ Increment i           ( i=i+1 )
    LOOP      \ Increment index.
              \ Loop back if
              \ index < limit
              \ else leave loop       ( i )
    DROP      \ Drop i                ( )
    ;         \ End definition
              \\ ok   \
```

```
14 INTEGERS
\\   1 2 3 4 5 6 7 8 9 10 11 12 13 14   ok   \


1  INTEGERS
\\   1   ok \

0   INTEGERS
\\   ok         \
```

This is all and more than all you need to know about counted loops for the moment. Please skip the rest of this lesson.

I recommended that you use `?DO`, use a positive limit, and set the starting index to zero:

+n 0 ?DO. ?DO

actually takes any limit and starting index: *limit start* `?DO`.
You may experiment by writing words that accept various values of *limit* and *start*.

We saw when commenting on INTEGERS that `?DO` removes the limit and the starting index from the stack
and that `LOOP` increments the index and compares it to the limit, leaving them loop, then the index equals the limit.

It is quite probable that your Forth keeps the limit and the index on Forth's second stack, called the Return Stack, and drops the limit and index from the return stack on leaving the loop.

This likelihood results in rules about using the return stack that I may discuss later.

`?DO` checks, if the limit and the starting index are equal, skipping the loop entirely if they are.

The word `DO` acts like `?DO` but doesn't check if the limit and the starting index are equal.
`DO` may be a tiny bit faster than `?DO`, but a condition like `0  0  DO  ...  LOOP` will likely give you more than you bargained for.

It returns the current loop index.
This is sometimes useful.

For example one could have defined:

```
: INTEGERS ( +n -- )
    1+ 1 ?DO I . LOOP ;

7 integers
\\ 1 2 3 4 5 6 7  ok
```

This program, translated from a famous book also uses `I`:

```
\ Power
\ after Kernighan and Ritchie,
\ The C Programming Language, 2nd ed., pp. 24-25
\ Raise base to n-th power; n >= 0
: power   ( base n -- base**n )
   1 SWAP 0 ?DO OVER * LOOP  NIP ;
```

Can you work it out?

```
\ Test power
: test   ( -- )
   10 0 ?DO  CR I .  2 I power .  -3 I power .  LOOP ;
```

J returns the index of the next *outer* loop when counted loops are nested in the same word.
This is useful for stepping through two-dimensional arrays:

```
\ Display indexes of a 2D array
: INDEXES   ( rows columns -- )
   SWAP            ( columns rows )
   0 ?DO           \ For number of rows
      CR           \ CR goes to next line
      DUP          \ DUPlicate columns
      0 ?DO        \ For number of rows
         J .       \ Display row index
         I .       \ Display column index
         SPACE     \ SPACE displays a space
      LOOP         \ End of inner loop
   LOOP ;          \ End of outer loop
```

```
3 4 INDEXES   \\ 0 0  0 1  0 2  0 3          \
              \\ 1 0  1 1  1 2  1 3          \
              \\ 2 0  2 1  2 2  2 3   ok-1 \
```

LEAVE and UNLOOP EXIT exit a counted loop or counted loops "prematurely".
LEAVE immediately leaves the loop it is in.
UNLOOP EXIT exits the word it is in, and can exit a word with nested loops.
Here are some phrases to ponder, more for the advanced user:

DO ... IF LEAVE THEN ... LOOP

DO ... IF UNLOOP EXIT THEN ... LOOP

DO ... DO... IF UNLOOP UNLOOP EXIT THEN... LOOP... LOOP

The phrase *n* +LOOP changes the loop index by *n*.
n can be positive or negative, permitting stepping up or stepping down through the loop.
Depending on whether it's up or down, the ending conditions, I think, "equal or greater than" or "less than".

Try if you like:

```
: LOOPY ( limit start step -- )
   ROT ROT ?DO I . DUP +LOOP DROP ;
```

```
10 0  1 LOOPY
\\   0 1 2 3 4 5 6 7 8 9  ok-1  \
```

```
0 10 -1 LOOPY
\\   10 9 8 7 6 5 4 3 2 1 0  ok  \
```

```
10 0  2 LOOPY
\\   0 2 4 6 8  ok                \
```

```
0 10 -2 LOOPY
\\   10 8 6 4 2 0  ok             \
```

```
10 0  3 LOOPY
\\   3 6 9  ok                    \
```

```
0 10 -3 LOOPY
\\   10 7 4 1  ok                 \
```

n before +LOOP can vary within the loop.

Here is a cute definition by Wil Baden:

```
: SQRT    ( n1 -- n2 )
    0 TUCK   DO   1+  DUP 2* 1+  +LOOP ;
```

```
9 SQRT
```

```
.S
\\ DATA STACK top  3 0000:0003  ok-1 \
```

Didn't I ask you not to read this? I think you now may understand why –
more for the specialists.

BYE

Lesson 17 - *Source Files*

Words in this lesson: S" INCLUDED INCLUDE

This program comes from Leo and he said: "I think I shall write a little game now. Since the game will take a few lines, I will revise as I develop the game,
I'll put the *source code* in a file.
I'll write the code with a text editor and then *load* the source into Forth by entering:
S" *filename"* INCLUDED where *filename"* is the name of the file followed by a double quotation mark.

As I develop and correct my program, I will get in and out of Forth and go back to my text editor.
This isn't the most efficient way of developing a Forth program - Forth is an "integrated development environment" in which Forth and the source editor can work much more closely together
- but it will work regardless of any Forth implementation.

Since the game could use a little unpredictability, I'll need a "random number generator".
I'll put that in a file too, so you can test S" *filename"* INCLUDED. "

VFX prefers INCLUDE DRIVE:\PATH\FILENAME.f.

The random number generator in Leo Brodie's *Starting Forth* will be more than good enough for our purposes. Either type or copy and paste the following into a file that you name random.f. The code has a few words that I might explain in another lesson.

For now just copy the source from A-------------to A---------- into VFX

A--

```
\ to be copied into the file random.f at C:\FORTH_LITE
\ random.f
\ Simple random number generator
\ from Leo Brodie, _Starting Forth_
\ FIRST GENERATE A FOLDER FORTH_LITE on your PC
\ IN THE DOCUMENTS  FOLDER  C:\FORTH_LITE
\ send C:\FOTH_LITE to the desktop for easy
\ visibility / accessibility
\ right click and send to desktop
```

```
VARIABLE RND
\\ ok
\ Holds current result


\ Generate a random integer
: RANDOM  ( -- u )  RND @  31421 *  6927 +  DUP RND ! ;
\\ RANDOM is redefined  ok \

\ Return a random integer between 0 and u-1
: CHOOSE  ( u -- 0...u-1 )  RANDOM UM* NIP ;
\\  ok \

\ Initialize
: RANDOMIZE  ( -- )   TIME&DATE + + + + + RND ! ;
\\  ok \
\ end of to be copied into the file random.f
```

A--

Copy and paste into VFX for direct testing/execution in VFX will show:

```
\ random.f  ok
\ Simple random number generator  ok
\ from Leo Brodie, _Starting Forth_  ok
\ FIRST GENERATE A FOLDER SIMPLEFORTH IN THE DOCUMENTS
FOLDER  C:\SIMPLEFORTH  ok
\ send C:\SIMPLEFORTH to the desktop for easy
visibility / accessibility  ok
  ok
VARIABLE RND  \\ ok     \ Holds current result
RND is redefined  ok
  ok
\ Generate a random integer  ok
: RANDOM  ( -- u )   RND @  31421 *  6927 +  DUP RND ! ;
\\ RANDOM is redefined  ok \
RANDOM is redefined  ok
  ok
\ Return a random integer between 0 and u-1  ok
: CHOOSE  ( u -- 0...u-1 )  RANDOM UM* NIP ;        \\
ok \
CHOOSE is redefined  ok
  ok
\ Initialize  ok
: RANDOMIZE  ( -- )   TIME&DATE + + + + + RND ! ;  \\
ok \
RANDOMIZE is redefined  ok
```

All ok, so VFX should be ready now for direct execution

And now test:

```
100 CHOOSE .
\\   0  ok
\  up to 100, CHOOSE one, display and remove

100 CHOOSE .
\\   5  ok

100 CHOOSE .
\\ 96  ok

100 CHOOSE .
\\ 24  ok

100 CHOOSE .
\\ 31  ok  \
```

Now we have to store this onto your PC.

First we need to generate a new Folder.
Where? I suggest a clear location easy to find again.

Go in the File Manger to Computer Local Disk (C:)

Right click on Local Disk (C) and go to New Folder.
Give this folder the name FORTH_LITE

We now have the folder ready to store our own Forth programs into.

Find this folder, right click onto it and send to desktop (create shortcut)

Open Notepad/Wordpad via
START -> All Programs -> Acessories -> Notepad/Wordpad

As you will use this program later again, it might save time to send it as
Shortcut to the Desktop:
START -> All Programs -> Acessories -> Notepad/Wordpad -> send to
Desktop

Double click on the Notepad/Wordpad shortcut to start it.

Next copy the relevant lines from between A------ and A-----, but excluding
them,
paste into Notepad,

Save this file as random.f and as TEXT DOCUMENT.

Be careful some programs save it as random.f.txt – which will not work,
VFX cannot read such a file.

Open the shortcut `C:\FORTH_LITE` to check the file is there.

Now try:

INCLUDE C:\FORTH_LITE\random.f
\\ Including C:\FORTH_LITE
\\random.f   RND is redefined ok \

\ which means that loading the file from hard drive
works.

Now try the random Number Generator, and see the same program
executed giver different numbers.

100 CHOOSE .
\\ 59 ok
\ These are a run of

100 CHOOSE .
\\ 18 ok
\ random numbers to

100 CHOOSE .
\\ 85 ok
\ prove they vary

100 CHOOSE .
\\ 27 ok
\ from 1

100 CHOOSE .
\\ 51 ok

\ to 100

<u>**BYE**</u>

Lesson 18 *Game of Sticks*

Words in this lesson: CR   SPACE   SPACES   ."   .(

Writing the Game of Sticks did not take very long because it is copied, it is the game from David H. Ahl's *BASIC Computer Games*.

If you can find a copy of that book you might wish to compare the BASIC code for "23 Matches" with the Forth code for "Sticks."
Of course, it did not mean just sit down and write "Sticks" without changing things and testing words in the process.

"Sticks" uses a few words that haven't been formally introduced yet, but are really easy to understand. Send information to screen:

CR	(--)	sends cursor to the start of the next line.
SPACE	(--)	displays a space.
SPACES	(n --)	displays *n* spaces (SPACES isn't used in sticks.f).
." *text*"	(--)	displays the text; if used in definitions, remembers (compiles) *text* up to, but not including ". *text* is then displayed when the word being defined is executed.
.(*text*)	(--)	immediately displays *text* up to, not including) .

You don't see . (much.
I'll use it in the source for "Sticks" to give you an indication of how quickly Forth reads code.

Try:

```
.( Four score and seven years ago )
\\  Four score and seven years ago  ok  \

\ And as word definition
: brought  .( our fathers ) ." Forth on this
continent." ;
\\  our fathers  ok  \


brought
\\  Forth on this continent. ok  \
```

Immediate text and compiled text in combination

```
.( Our fathers brought ) brought
\\ Our fathers brought Forth on this continent. ok
```

Now type or copy and paste the following code into a file called sticks.f and first to check copy into VFX for direct execution:

```
A-------------------------------------------------------------
\ sticks.f
\ After "23 Matches" in Ahl, _Basic Computer Games_
\ Ahl attributes the original to Bob Albrecht

CR .( Reading sticks.fth)

\ random number generator
INCLUDE C:\FORTH_LITE\random.f
\ Rules of the game
: RULES  ( -- )
   CR ." Sticks"
   CR
   CR ." The game starts with 23 sticks.  "
      ." By turns, you and Forth take"
   CR ." from 1 to 3 sticks.  "
      ." Whoever takes the last stick loses."
   CR
   CR ." You take sticks by entering:  n STICKS"
   CR ." where n is 1, 2, or 3"
   CR ;

\ Display sticks

: .STICKS  ( n -- )  0 ?DO  ." |"  LOOP ;

\ Report remaining sticks
: LEFT  ( sticks taken -- left )
   -  DUP CR .STICKS SPACE DUP . ." left." ;

\ The fates of Forth
: YOU-WIN  ( sticks -- )  DROP  ." You win! " ;

: FORTH-WINS  ( sticks -- )
   ." Forth took " 1- .
   CR ." 1 left - sorry!" ;

: 4-PLAY  ( sticks -- left )
   ." Forth took " 3 CHOOSE 1+ DUP . LEFT ;

\ My esteemed opponent
: COMPUTER  ( sticks -- left| )
   CR
   DUP 1 = IF  YOU-WIN     ELSE
   DUP 5 < IF  FORTH-WINS  ELSE
            4-PLAY
          THEN THEN ;
```

```
\ First play
: COIN   ( 23 -- n )
   2 CHOOSE
   CR ." A coin has been flipped:  "
   IF   ." Heads, Forth is first."  COMPUTER
   ELSE ." Tails, you start."
   THEN ;

\ Confine n between min and max
: CLAMP   ( n min max -- n )  ROT MIN MAX ;

\ May take between 1 and 3 sticks, leaving at least 1
: LEGAL   ( sticks try -- sticks taken )
   OVER 1- 3 MIN  1 SWAP CLAMP ;

\ My play
: PROGRAMMER   ( sticks try - left )  LEGAL LEFT ;

\ 1 Round
: STICKS   ( sticks try -- left| ) PROGRAMMER COMPUTER ;

\ Alias for STICKS
: STICK   ( sticks try -- left| )  STICKS ;

: GAME   ( -- )
   RULES  23 DUP CR .STICKS  RANDOMIZE COIN ;

CR .( Ready.  To play, enter: GAME)
```

A---

The answer from VFX will be:

```
\ sticks.f  ok
\ After "23 Matches" in Ahl, _Basic Computer Games_  ok
\ Ahl attributes the original to Bob Albrecht  ok
  ok
CR .( Reading sticks.fth)
Reading sticks.fth ok
  ok
\ random number generator  ok
INCLUDE C:\SIMPLEFORTH\random.f
Including C:\SIMPLEFORTH\random.f
RND is redefined  ok
  ok
\ Rules of the game  ok
: RULES   ( -- )
RULES is redefined
   CR ." Sticks"
   CR
   CR ." The game starts with 23 sticks.  "
      ." By turns, you and Forth take"
```

```
       CR ." from 1 to 3 sticks.  "
          ." Whoever takes the last stick loses."
       CR
       CR ." You take sticks by entering:  n STICKS"
       CR ." where n is 1, 2, or 3"
       CR ;  ok
    ok
\ Display sticks  ok
: .STICKS  ( n -- )  0 ?DO  ." |"  LOOP ;
.STICKS is redefined  ok
    ok
\ Report remaining sticks  ok
: LEFT  ( sticks taken -- left )
LEFT is redefined
    - DUP CR .STICKS SPACE DUP . ." left." ;  ok
    ok
\ The fates of Forth  ok
: YOU-WIN  ( sticks -- )  DROP  ." You win! " ;
YOU-WIN is redefined  ok
: FORTH-WINS  ( sticks -- )
FORTH-WINS is redefined
   ." Forth took " 1- .
   CR ." 1 left - sorry!" ;  ok
: 4-PLAY  ( sticks -- left )
4-PLAY is redefined
   ." Forth took " 3 CHOOSE 1+ DUP . LEFT ;  ok
    ok
\ My esteemed opponent  ok
: COMPUTER  ( sticks -- left| )
COMPUTER is redefined
   CR
   DUP 1 = IF  YOU-WIN      ELSE
   DUP 5 < IF  FORTH-WINS  ELSE
               4-PLAY
          THEN THEN ;  ok
    ok
\ First play  ok
: COIN  ( 23 -- n )
COIN is redefined
   2 CHOOSE
   CR ." A coin has been flipped:  "
   IF  ." Heads, Forth is first." COMPUTER
   ELSE ." Tails, you start."
   THEN ;  ok
    ok
\ Confine n between min and max  ok
: CLAMP  ( n min max -- n )  ROT MIN MAX ;
CLAMP is redefined  ok
```

```
  ok
\ May take between 1 and 3 sticks, leaving at least 1
ok
: LEGAL   ( sticks try -- sticks taken )
LEGAL is redefined
   OVER 1- 3 MIN  1 SWAP CLAMP ;    ok
  ok
\ My play  ok
: PROGRAMMER  ( sticks try - left )  LEGAL LEFT ;
PROGRAMMER is redefined  ok
  ok
\ 1 Round  ok
: STICKS  ( sticks try -- left| )  PROGRAMMER COMPUTER
;
STICKS is redefined  ok
\ Alias for STICKS  ok
: STICK  ( sticks try -- left| )  STICKS ;
STICK is redefined  ok
  ok
: GAME  ( -- )
GAME is redefined
   RULES  23 DUP CR .STICKS  RANDOMIZE COIN ;   ok
  ok
CR .( Ready.  To play, enter: GAME)
Ready.  To play, enter: GAME ok
```

Now enter GAME

```
\\ Sticks
\\
\\ The game starts with 23 sticks.  By turns, you and
Forth take
\\ from 1 to 3 sticks.  Whoever takes the last stick
loses.
\\
\\ You take sticks by entering:  n STICKS
\\ where n is 1, 2, or 3
\\
\\ |||||||||||||||||||||||
\\ A coin has been flipped:  Tails, you start. ok-1
```

And enter x sticks ***and CR***
and so on until the end

You can Restart the game by entering GAME

Now save the game into a file
Open Notepad   START -> All Programs -> Acessories -> Notepad

copy the relevant lines inside A------- to A-------into Notepad, save the file as sticks.f into the folder C:\FORTH_LIT

For people who have issues with notepad, try Notepad++, I used it just now.

Check if the file sticks.f is in the folder

Now try:

```
INCLUDE C:\FORTH_LITE\sticks.f
```

And VFX will show

```
\\   Including C:\FORTH_LITE\sticks.f
\ and VFX will answer
\\    Reading sticks.fth
\\    Including C:\SIMPLEFORTH\random.f
\\    RND is redefined
\\    RULES is redefined
\\    .STICKS is redefined
\\    LEFT is redefined
\\    YOU-WIN is redefined
\\    FORTH-WINS is redefined
\\    4-PLAY is redefined
\\    COMPUTER is redefined
\\    COIN is redefined
\\    CLAMP is redefined
\\    LEGAL is redefined
\\    PROGRAMMER is redefined
\\    STICKS is redefined
\\    STICK is redefined
\\    GAME is redefined
\\    Ready.  To play, enter: GAME ok
\ less lines possibly, depending on status
```

Enter GAME to start
And then N sticks

Homework: write your own version of Sticks e.g. more sticks to take, start with more sticks or find another easy game in Basic and re-program in Forth.

BYE

Lesson 19 - *More to Display*

Words in this lesson: PAGE   AT-XY   .R   MS

Sticks.f used CR SPACE SPACES . ." . (for displaying on the screen.
Here are three additional display words:

PAGE   (--)   clears the screen and puts
                                the cursor in the top left corner.

AT-XY   (col row --) moves the cursor to *col row*. Top left is 0 0

.

.R   (n u --)   displays the signed integer *n* right aligned in
                                a field *u* spaces wide.
                                .R is often used to display numbers in columns.

Not technically a display word but useful in this context and does not really
fit anywhere else:

MS   (+n --)   Wait for +*n* milliseconds. So,1000ms means 1
sec

Try:

```
PAGE  30 12 AT-XY .( FORTH_LITE )
\ clears page, displays FORTH_LITE in row 12 column 30
                    ^
```

```
PAGE  CR 1 3 .R  CR 12 3 .R  CR 123 3 .R
\\    1
\\    12
\\    123 ok
```

```
PAGE  33 12 2DUP AT-XY  100 5 .R  2000 MS  AT-XY 1 5 .R
\\  100      1 ok  \ at x y
```

Homework: Improve Sticks by using words introduced in this lesson.

BYE

Lesson 20 - *Data on the Return Stack*

Words in this lesson: >R   R@   R>   2>R   2R@   2R>

We have explained the Data Stack (in short "stack") already. You will occasionally find it very convenient to be able to put a stack item temporarily in another place.

"Another" place is the return stack. Your Forth almost certainly uses the return stack for its own purposes, so *your* use of the return stack must follow certain rigid rules:

Data put on the return stack must be taken back *within the same word*.

Data put on the return stack *outside* a ?DO (DO) ... LOOP (+LOOP) cannot be accessed *within* the loop.

Data put on the return stack *within* a ?DO (DO) ... LOOP (+LOOP) must be taken back *before* leaving the loop.

Data cannot be on the return stack when executing I or J in a loop.

The following words and descriptions are the needed data and return stack words:

  (S: ... -- ...) shows the (data) stack effect

  (R: ... -- ...) shows the return stack effect.

>R
(S: x --)   (R: -- x)
\ moves item *x* from the data stack to the return stack.

R@
(R: x -- x)(S: -- x)
\ just copies item *x* from the return stack to the stack.

R>
(R: x --)   (S: -- x)
moves *x* from the return stack to the stack.

2>R
(S: x1 x2 --) (R: -- x1 x2)
\ moves *x1 and x2* from the stack to the return stack.

2R@
```
( R: x1 x2 -- x1 x2 )( S: -- x1 s2 )
```
\ copies *x1 and x2* from the return stack to the stack.

2R>
```
( R: x1 x2 -- )          ( S: -- x1 x2)
```
moves *x1 and x2* from the return stack to the stack.

We will use return stack words in future lessons. The use will simplify coding. You won't find anything like this:

```
\ pascal.f
\ Pascal's Triangle
: POSITION  ( row -- )  CR  33 SWAP 2 *  - SPACES ;
: PAS ( 0 ... 0 -- 0 ... 0 )
   0 >R
   BEGIN  OVER + >R  DUP 0= UNTIL
   BEGIN  R> DUP WHILE  DUP 4 .R  REPEAT ;
: PASS  ( -- )
   0 1 0
   13 0 ?DO  DUP POSITION  >R  PAS  R>  1+  LOOP  DROP ;
: PAX  ( 0 ... 0 -- )  DROP BEGIN 0= UNTIL ;
: PASCAL  ( -- )  PASS PAX ;


BYE
```

Lesson 21 *Named Storage*

Words in this lesson: CONSTANT   VARIABLE   U.   U.R
!   @   +!   ?

Stack items are anonymous, documented only by the stack effect comments that you are urged but not required to write.

Forth can also name data. We start with two words:

x CONSTANT *name*   defines the word *name* (-- x) that returns the constant *x* and uses a memory location in free space

VARIABLE *name*   defines the word *name* (-- addr) that will return the memory address *addr*, where there is reserved space for one cell of data
(remember that a stack item is the size of one cell).

Your Forth dictionary probably comes with the constants TRUE and FALSE, which return the well-formed flags with all bits set for TRUE and all bit reset for FALSE respectively.
If not, they are easy to define (I think we've defined them twice before).

Try:

```
0 CONSTANT FALSE
\ use the value 0 and define
\ the CONSTANT FALSE as 0

FALSE FALSE = CONSTANT TRUE   \

FALSE .
\\   0  ok
\ put false on the stack, and display it

TRUE .
\\ -1  ok
\   put true on the stack, and display it

123 CONSTANT EASY
\ I need 123 defined as the
\ CONSTANT with the name EASY

EASY .
\\   123  ok
\   EASY, display the value of
\   this constant, it is 123
```

We defined the variable RND in random.f
Let's define another variable and display its address.

Try:

VARIABLE x
\\ ok \
\ define a variable named x

x U.
\\ 4592668 ok
\ x has a memory address, show with U. where it is located

U. displays an *unsigned integer.*
Memory addresses are always positive integers.

U. (u --) displays the unsigned integer *u.*

U.R (u n --) displays the unsigned integer *u* right aligned in a field *n* spaces wide, very good for tables

10 U.
\\ 10 ok
\ display the unsigned integer 10

10 20 U.R
\\   10 ok
\ display unsigned integer 10 in right aligned 20 block

A constant's value doesn't change (in Forth one can change anything, but this is Forth LITE for starters).
A variable name returns an address at which a value can be "stored" and from which a copy of the stored value can be "fetched".
To change what is fetched from a variable's address, store a different value there. The words for storing and fetching are:

! (x addr --) stores *x* at the address *addr.*

@ (addr -- x) fetches a copy of *x* from the address *addr.*

+! (x addr --) adds *x* to the value at *addr.* For counters for example

Try:

VARIABLE y
\\ ok
\ define the VARIABLE y

y U.
\\ 4592668 ok

```
\  which memory location is it?
\ (the address value will probably be different for
you)
```

50 y !
```
\\ ok
\ 50 to be allocated to address at y and stored there
```

y @ .
```
\\ 50   ok
\ y is a variable, and at this location
\ which value is stored there? Display.
```

100 y !
```
\  now 100 to be stored at y
```

y @ .
```
\  y has what stored at this location? Display it
```

1 y +!
```
\\  ok
\  1 to be added to the address y value at y
```

y @ .
```
\\  101  ok
\  check result, 101, that's what we expected
```

Most Forths have a separate word for @ .:

? (addr --) displays the value at *addr*.

Try:

VARIABLE z
```
\\ ok
\  define variable z
```

7 z !
```
\\ ok
\  7 at z store
```

z ?
```
\\ 7  ok
\  z has which contents ? OK it is 7
```

VARIABLE w
```
\\ ok
\ define w
```

11 w !
```
\\ ok
\ 11 at w store
```

```
w ?
\\ 11   ok
\ w contents show?
```

```
z @ w @ z ! w !
\\ ok
\ contents of z (7) onto stack (7),
\ contents of w (11) onto stack (11)
\ TOS (11) at z store, TOS now
\ (7) at w store
```

```
z ?
\\ 11   ok   \
```

```
w ?
\\ 7   ok   \
```

So we swapped the values at w and z. Now the same written as a new word:

```
\ Exchange values of two variables
```

```
: VSWAP   ( addr1 addr2 -- )   2DUP 2>R   @ SWAP @   R> !
R> ! ;
\\ ok   \
```

```
w ?
\\    7   ok   \
```

```
z ?
\\ 11   ok   \
```

```
w z VSWAP
\\         ok   \
```

```
w ?
\\ 11   ok   \
```

```
z ?
\\    7   ok   \
```

Addresses are cell-sized data. Add a level of indirection for Variables

```
VARIABLE OLD
\\ ok
\ define a VARIABLE
\ with the name OLD
```

```
VARIABLE NEW
\\ ok
\ define a VARIABLE with the name NEW
```

VARIABLE INDIRECTION
\\ ok
\ define a VARIABLE with the name INDIRECTION

67 OLD !
\\ ok
\ 67 into OLD store

70 NEW !
\\ ok
\ 70 into NEW store

OLD INDIRECTION !
\\ ok
\ value in OLD (67) into INDIECTION location store

\ EMIT displays a character

INDIRECTION @ @ EMIT
\\ C ok
\ Get address at
\ INDIRECTION, then get
\ value at that address,
\ then EMIT the value

NEW INDIRECTION !
\\ ok
\ Store the address of
\ NEW at INDIRECTION

INDIRECTION @ @ EMIT
\\ F ok
\ Now the value stored
\ at NEW is EMITted

You might want to draw a picture of what happens here

<u>BYE</u>

Lesson 22 - *Accessing Memory Part 1*

Words in this lesson: UNUSED   CELLS

In the last lesson, we learned how to name and access a cell of data in memory by using ! +! @.

In this and the next few lessons we'll work with groups of cells in memory. Much of the discussion will be applicable when working with data that may be more or less than a cell in size.

Forth systems tend to be small and only use a small part of the computer. What the Forth system doesn't use, is available to the programmer. Your system may have the word UNUSED that tells how many memory addresses are currently available for data.

UNUSED (-- u) returns *u*, the number of addresses still available.

Try:

UNUSED U.
\\ 7555676 ok-1   \
\ a lot of unused memory space here

As you add words and data structures to your program, the amount of unused space gets smaller.

Try:

UNUSED U.
\\ 7555 676 ok-1   \
\ let us check what happens, here we start

VARIABLE x
\\ ok-1   \
\ variable x is defined

UNUSED U.
\\ 7555 628 ok-1   \

\   number is getting smaller

Variable A

UNUSED U.
\\ 7555 580 ok-1   \

Since we've been working with cell-sized data, we now introduce a new word:

CELLS (n1 -- n2) returns *n2*, the number of address units
in *n1* cells.

It's likely that a cell occupies 2 address units if you have a 16-bit Forth and 4 address units if you have a 32-bit Forth. I say address *units*, since the *address* of the cell is the address of the first address unit occupied by the cell.

To see for yourself, try:

1 CELLS .
\\   4   ok-1   \

2 CELLS .
\\   8   ok-1   \

10 CELLS .
\\ 40   ok-1   \

To see how many cells could fit in currently unused memory, try:

UNUSED 1 CELLS / .
\\ 1 888 895   ok-1   \

\   a lot of typing to fill this up
\   with words and data

<u>BYE</u>

Lesson 23 - *Accessing Memory Part 2*

Words in this lesson: `CREATE`   `HERE`   `ALLOT`   `ERASE`
`CELL+`

Let us claim some unused memory.

`CREATE` **name**   defines *name*, which returns a memory address.

`HERE` (`-- addr`) returns the next free memory address.

`ALLOT` (`n -- `)   reserves *n* address units of memory.

`CREATE` *name* resembles `VARIABLE` *name* but doesn't reserve space. To
reserve space after `CREATE` *name*, you `ALLOT` it.
The first address that is reserved is the address returned by `HERE`.

Try:

```
CREATE ITEMS
\\   ok           \
```

```
ITEMS U.
\\   5019008   ok   \
```

```
HERE U.
\\   5019008   ok   \
```

```
1 CELLS ALLOT
\\   ok           \
```

```
HERE U.
\\   5019012   ok
\ + 1 x 4 = 4
```

```
4 CELLS ALLOT
\\   ok           \
```

```
HERE U.
\\   5019028   ok
\ + 4 x 4 = 16
```

A word that combines `CREATE` and `ALLOT` can be defined to make life
easier.

Try:

```
\ Reserve n address units starting at name
\ n BUFFER: name
: BUFFER:   ( n -- )   CREATE ALLOT ;
\\ ok   \
```

```
4 20 + CELLS BUFFER: BLACKBIRDS
\\ ok
\ here BLACKBIRD is defined
```

```
BLACKBIRDS 24 CELLS DUMP
\\  0046:1420  00 00 00 00 00 00 00 00  00 00 00 00 00
00 00 \\  00  ................  \96 bytes
\\  0046:1430  00 00 00 00 00 00 00 00  00 00 00 00 00
00 00 \\  00  ................  \divided x 4
\\  0046:1440  00 00 00 00 00 00 00 00  00 00 00 00 00
00 00 \\  00  ................  \24 cells
\\  0046:1450  00 00 00 00 00 00 00 00  00 00 00 00 00
00 00 \\  00  ................  \ of 4 bytes
\\  0046:1460  00 00 00 00 00 00 00 00  00 00 00 00 00
00 00 \\  00  ................  \
\\  0046:1470  00 00 00 00 00 00 00 00  00 00 00 00 00
00 00 \\  00  ................  \
\\  ok
```

The word BUFFER: could be "enhanced" by making it initialize (typically set to zeroes) the space ALLOTed, but we'll leave it as it is and initialize with in separate step:

ERASE (a u --) sets the contents u addresses starting from a to zero.

Try:

```
BLACKBIRDS 24 CELLS ERASE
\\  ok  \\
```

```
BLACKBIRDS 24 CELLS DUMP
\\  004C:9870  00 00 00 00 00 00 00 00  00 00 00 00 00
00 00 \\  00  ................
\\  004C:9880  00 00 00 00 00 00 00 00  00 00 00 00 00
00 00 \\  00  ................
\\  004C:9890  00 00 00 00 00 00 00 00  00 00 00 00 00
00 00 \\  00  ................
\\  004C:98A0  00 00 00 00 00 00 00 00  00 00 00 00 00
00 00 \\  00  ................
\\  004C:98B0  00 00 00 00 00 00 00 00  00 00 00 00 00
00 00 \\  00  ................
\\  004C:98C0  00 00 00 00 00 00 00 00  00 00 00 00 00
00 00 \\  00  ................
\\  ok
```

Once you have CREATEd (that is, named) and ALLOTed space in memory, you can ! (store), +! (add to or "plus" store), @ (fetch), and ? (question) data from within that space by calculating the particular address needed.

The starting address is returned by *name*. The addresses of the following cells are calculated by adding *n* CELLS to the starting address.

Given 5 cells starting at ITEMS *try:*

```
ITEMS U.
\\   5019072   ok   \

50 ITEMS  !
\\   ok              \

ITEMS  ?
\\   50   ok         \

ITEMS 0 CELLS + U.
\\   5019072   ok

ITEMS 0 CELLS + ?
\\   50   ok         \

ITEMS 1 CELLS + U.
\\   5019076   ok  \

95 ITEMS 1 CELLS + !
\\   ok              \

ITEMS 1 CELLS + ?
\\   95   ok         \

ITEMS 2 CELLS + U.
\\   5019080   ok  \

77 ITEMS 2 CELLS + !
\\   ok              \

ITEMS 2 CELLS + ?
\\   77   ok         \

23 ITEMS 2 CELLS + +!
\\   ok              \

ITEMS 2 CELLS + ?         \
\   100   ok         \
```

There are many ways of not having to repeatedly write *n* CELLS to calculate memory addresses. Here are two simple ways:

Try:

```
\ Return address of cell n from addr
: TH  ( addr n -- n-addr )   CELLS + ;
\\   ok   \

ITEMS  ?
\\   50   ok   \
```

```
ITEMS 0 TH ?
\\  50  ok  \

ITEMS 3 TH U.
\\  5019084  ok  \

33 ITEMS 3 TH !
\\  ok            \

ITEMS 3 TH ?
\\  0  ok         \
```

```
\ Return address of cell n of ITEMS
: ITEM  ( n -- addr )  CELLS ITEMS + ;
\\  ok  \
```

```
ITEMS ?
\\  50  ok   \

0 ITEM ?
\\  50  ok   \

25 4 ITEM !
\\  ok        \

4 ITEM ?
\\  25  ok   \
```

The word for going from one cell address to the next is:

CELL+ (addr1 -- addr2) adds 1 CELLS to *addr1*.

Try:

```
\ Display n cells beginning at addr
: .CELLS  ( addr n -- )
    0 ?DO  DUP ?  CELL+  LOOP  DROP ;
\\  ok  \
```

```
ITEMS 5 .CELLS
\\  50 95 100 0 25  ok  \
```

```
\ Sum of n cells beginning at addr

: SUM-CELLS  ( addr n -- sum )
   0 ROT ROT  0 ?DO  DUP >R  @ +  R> CELL+  LOOP  DROP ;
\\  ok  \
```

```
ITEMS 5 SUM-CELLS
\\  ok-1  \
```

For another definition of SUM-CELLS *try:*

```
: UNDER+  ( n1 x n2 -- n1+n2 x ) ROT + SWAP ;
\\  ok-1 \
```

```
: SUM-CELLS   ( addr n -- sum )
   0 ROT ROT  0 ?DO  DUP @ UNDER+  CELL+  LOOP  DROP ;
\\  ok-1  \
```

```
ITEMS 5 SUM-CELLS
\\  ok-2  \
```

Homework: write yet another definition of SUM-CELLS *by using*

```
: @+  ( addr1 -- addr2 n ) DUP CELL+  SWAP @ ;
\\ ok-2 \
```

and any other words you know or care to define.

BYE

Lesson 24 - *Accessing Memory Part 3*

Words in this lesson: ,

After a long lesson a short one on a short word:

, (x --) reserves a cell of memory and stores *x* in it.

Try:

```
: TH   ( addr1 n -- addr2 )   CELLS + ;
\\ TH is redefined  ok-2  \
\ Powers of 2 from 2^0 to 2^8
```

```
CREATE 2^  1 ,  2 ,  4 ,  8 ,  16 ,  32 ,  64 ,  128 ,
256 ,
\\ ok-2 \
```

```
2^ ?
\\   ok-1  \
```

```
2^ CELL+ ?
\\   2  ok      \
```

```
2^ 2 CELLS + ?
\\   4  ok      \
```

```
2^ 0 TH ?
\\  1  ok      \
```

```
2^ 1 TH ?
\\  2  ok      \
```

```
2^ 2 TH ?
\\  4  ok      \
```

```
2^ 8 TH ?
\\  256  ok  \
```

A word by Wil Baden can make this procedure even nicer.

Try:
```
\ "commas" by Wil Baden
```

```
: ,S  ( x1 ... xn n -- )
   BEGIN ?DUP WHILE  DUP ROLL , 1-  REPEAT ;
\\  ok \
```

```
\ Redefine   2^ 0 1 2 3  4  5  6   7   8
CREATE 2^       1 2 4 8 16 32 64 128 256   9 ,S
\\ 2^ is redefined  ok  \
```

```
: ?+   ( addr1 -- addr2 )   DUP ? CELL+ ;
\\  ok  \


2^  ?+ ?+ ?+ ?+ ?+ ?+ ?+ ?+ ?
\\  1 2 4 8 16 32 64 128 256  ok  \
```

BYE

Lesson 25 - *Decimal - Hexadecimal - Binary*

Words in this lesson: BASE   DECIMAL   HEX   DUMP

Mostly we've been using ordinary-looking numbers like 5 12 33.
These are decimal - or base 10 - numbers represented with the 10 digits
from 0 to 9.
In Forth, numbers can be entered or displayed in any base from 2 to 36
(the computer stores the numbers in binary - base 2).

The base in which numbers are input and displayed is stored in a variable:

BASE (-- addr) holds the current base.

Forth has words for making the base decimal or hexadecimal:

DECIMAL (--) stores 10 (decimal) in BASE

HEX (--) stores 16 (decimal) in BASE

Try:

DECIMAL
\\ ok
\ work with decimal numbers

16 .
\\ 16 ok
\ 16 has to be displayed as 16 in decimal

16 HEX .
\\ 10 ok
\ 16 in decimal changed to 10 in HEX
\ For your reference a list in decimal and hex and
binary

\ decimal
\ 0 1 2 3 4 5 6 7 8 9 10 11 12 13 14 15 16 18
18 19 20   \

\ hex
\ 0 1 2 3 4 5 6 7 8 9 A B C D E F 10 11
12 13 14   \

\ binary
0-0000   1-0001   2-0010   3-0011   4-0100   5-0101 6-
0110
7-0111   8-1000   9-1001   A-1010   B-1011   C-1100   D-
1101   E-1110 F-1111 10-0001 0000 11-0001 0001 12-0001
0010\

FF .
\\ FF ok
\ in hex mode from before, so FF
\ is displayed

FF DECIMAL .
\\ 255 ok
\ in hex mode, so ff onto stack,
\ then switch to decimal and
\ the FF on stack is displayed as 255

1024 .
\\ 1024 ok
\ in decimal mode, so 1024 is displayed

1024 HEX .
\\ 400   ok-1
\ 1024 decimal onto stack,
\ switch to hex, display as 400 now

DECIMAL
\\ ok-1

Playing around with examples sometimes leaves the stack in a non-empty state – careful, here ok-1

.
\\ 1024 ok
\ an additional . prints the value

\ and the ok is back,
\ stack is empty

Usually the base is decimal
but hexadecimal with its base of 16, where digits range from 0 to F - is very convenient in computing, because a hexadecimal digit represents
4 bits (0=0001, 1=0001, 2=0010, 3=0011 ... F=1111).

That means that 8 bits can be represented by 2 hexadecimal digits,
16 bits by 4 hexadecimal digits,
32 bits by 8 hexadecimal digits, and so on.

This grouping of bits makes it often easier to understand what's going on inside a computer. The word DUMP reports values in hexadecimal:

DUMP (addr u --) displays the contents of u consecutive addresses beginning at addr. The display depends in general on the implementation. You'll often see on each line an address, then 16 2-digit hexadecimal numbers representing the contents of 16 addresses, then the ASCII equivalents of the same contents so you can spot words for example.

To make our life easier, we can write words that restore the current base after displaying in another base.

Try:

```
\ Display as an unsigned hexadecimal number
: H.  ( n -- )  BASE @ >R  HEX U.  R> BASE ! ;
\\  ok  \
```

```
\ Display as an unsigned binary number
: B.  ( n -- )  BASE @ >R  2 BASE ! U.  R> BASE ! ;
\\  ok  \
```

```
\ Display as an unsigned decimal number
\ as D. is already used in Forth D#
: D#.  ( n -- )  BASE @ >R  DECIMAL .  R> BASE ! ;
\\  ok  \
```

```
\ Display a number as decimal, hexadecimal, binary
: DHB.  ( n -- )  DUP D#.  DUP H.  B. ;
\\  ok  \
```

```
DECIMAL
\\  ok
\ define input as DECIMAL
```

```
1 DHB.
\\  1   1   1  ok
\ display options of the number 1
\ in decimal, hex, binary
```

```
2 DHB.
\\  2   2  10  ok
\  for 2
```

```
3 DHB.
\\  3      3      11  ok   \
```

```
4 DHB.
\\  4      4     100  ok   \
```

```
10 DHB.
\\ 10      A    1010  ok \
```

```
15 DHB.
\\ 15      F    1111  ok \
```

```
16 DHB.
\\ 16     10   1 0000  ok \
```

```
1023 DHB.
\\ 1023 3FF  11 1111 1111  ok \
```

```
1024 DHB.
\\ 1024   400   100 0000 0000   ok  \
```

HEX
```
\\   ok     \
\   define input as Hexadecimal
\   and all 3 outputs dec, hex, bin
\  reformatted for easier readability
```

```
1 DHB.
\\   1           1                       1   ok  \
```

```
2 DHB.
\\   2           2                      10   ok  \
```

```
A DHB.
\\  10           A                    1010   ok  \
```

```
F DHB.
\\  15           F                    1111   ok  \
```

```
10 DHB.
\\  16          10                 1 0000   ok  \
```

```
FF DHB.
\\ 255          FF              1111 1111   ok  \
```

```
100 DHB.
\\ 256         100           1 0000 0000   ok  \
```

```
1000 DHB.
\\ 4096       1000        1 0000 0000 0000   ok  \
```

```
FFFF DHB.
\\ 65535   FFFF   1111 1111 1111 1111   ok  \
```

```
10000 DHB.
\\ 65536 10000 1 0000 0000 0000 0000   ok  \
```

I hope the formatting works out for reading on your display

Now create 3 cells, and store 10, 100 and 1000 into them and check

```
CREATE POTS   3 CELLS ALLOT
\\   ok   \
\
```

```
10 POTS !
\\   ok   \
```

```
100 POTS CELL+ !
\\   ok   \
```

```
1000 POTS 2 CELLS + !
\\  ok  \
```

Check if the values are in these 3 cells:

```
POTS ?
\\   10  ok  \
```

```
POTS CELL+ ?
\\  100  ok  \
```

```
POTS 2 CELLS + ?
\\ 1000  ok  \
```

```
DECIMAL
\\ set Input to DECIMAL
```

```
POTS 3 CELLS DUMP
\\ 004C:9720  10 00 00 00 00
\\ 01 00 00  00 10 00 00 04 44 55 4D ..DUM   ok \
```

Now display the contents in decimal, hex and binary

```
POTS @ DHB.
\\   16    10           1 0000 ok \
```

```
POTS CELL+ @ DHB.
\\  256   100       1 0000 0000 ok \
```

```
POTS 2 CELLS + @ DHB.
\\ 4096 1000  1 0000 0000 0000 ok \
```

```
2 BASE !
\\  ok  \  set to base 2, binary as input
```

```
1 DHB.
\\  1 1   1  ok \
```

```
10 DHB.
\\  2 2  10  ok \
```

```
11 DHB.
\\  3 3  11  ok \
```

```
100 DHB.
\\  4 4 100  ok \
```

```
DECIMAL
\\  ok  \
\ set back to DECIMAL
```

__BYE__

Lesson 26 - *Booleans and Bits*

Words in this lesson: `AND   OR   XOR   0<>   INVERT`
`2*   2/   LSHIFT   RSHIFT`

If you want to work with logic decisions in your software, you will have to change from bytes, words, cells to single bits. Booleans is short for Boolean algebra, where you have AND, OR, XOR and INVERT as the basic operators:

For beginners some examples of the operators AND, OR, XOR, INV:

If I have the car key, **AND** there is petrol in the car, I can drive away
If I have the key **OR** I can find the reserve key, I can drive away
If we want to drive away, A **XOR** B can sit in the driver seat (not both)
INV flips a bit from 0 to 1 or 1 to 0 for easier processing later.

Our examples show only the results dealing with 2 inputs, but you can build as well Boolean functions with any number of inputs, the result stays the same:

AND – all inputs have to be 1 to result in 1
OR   - at least one input has to be 1 to result in output
XOR – only one input can be 1 to have 1 as output

Forth's "logical operators" are all *bit operators*.

```
AND ( x1 x2 -- x3 )
\ 0A AND 0B = 0Y, 1A AND 0B = 0Y,
\ 0A AND 1B = 0Y, 1A AND 1B = 1Y

OR ( x1 x2 -- x3 )
\ 0A OR  0B = 0Y, 1A OR  0B = 1Y,
\ 0A OR  1B = 1Y, 1A OR  1B = 1Y

XOR ( x1 x2 -- x3 )
\ 0A XOR 0B = 0Y, 1A XOR 0B = 1Y,
\ 0A XOR 1B = 1Y, 1A XOR 1B = 0Y

INV ( x1 - x2 )
\ 0A INV = 1Y
\ 1A INV = 0Y
```

Try:

```
1 1 AND .
\\  1  ok
\ both are 1, so 1 is the result
```

```
1 0 AND .
\\  0  ok
\ the other is 0, so output 0


0 1 AND .
\\  0  ok  \

0 0 AND .
\\  0  ok  \

1 1 OR .
\\  1  ok
\ 1 1 is 1, as the next 2

1 0 OR .
\\  1  ok  \

0 1 OR .
\\  1  ok  \

0 0 OR .
\\  0  ok
\ only if none is 1 then result is 0

1 1 XOR .
\\  0  ok
\ only 1 if one of the 2 inputs
\ exclusively is 1 then the result is 1

1 0 XOR .
\\  1  ok  \

0 1 XOR .
\\  1  ok  \

0 0 XOR .
\\  0  ok  \
```

And to display it differently:

```
: B.  ( u -- )  BASE @ >R  2 BASE ! U.  R> BASE ! ;
\\  ok  \

1 DUP B. 2 DUP B. AND B.   \\  1  10   0  ok  \
1 DUP B. 2 DUP B. OR  B.   \\  1  10  11  ok  \
1 DUP B. 2 DUP B. XOR B.   \\  1  10  11  ok  \
1 DUP B. 3 DUP B. AND B.   \\  1  11   1  ok  \
1 DUP B. 3 DUP B. OR  B.   \\  1  11  11  ok  \
1 DUP B. 3 DUP B. XOR B.   \\  1  11  10  ok  \
```

Often you will use flags on the stack for such calculations.
Any non-zero flag is treated as true, but 1 2 AND would leave zero, 01
AND 10, so it's wise to AND only well-formed flags.

You can make a flag well formed with 0<>:

0<> (x -- flag) \ Does x not equal zero?

A definition of 0<> might be:

```
: 0<>  ( x -- flag )  0= 0= ;
\\  0<> is redefined  ok  \
```

Try:

```
1 2 AND .
\\  0  ok
\   uses 01 and 10 for AND, so
\\  1 AND 0 = 0

1 0<> 2 0<> AND .
\\ -1  ok
\   this is the correct answer
\   two well formed flags build before the AND
```

```
\ A year is a leap year if:
\ it's divisible by 4 but not by 100
\ or it's divisible by 400
: LEAP ( year -- flag )
\ nonzero flag means a leap year
    DUP 4 MOD 0=  OVER 100 MOD AND
    SWAP 400 MOD 0= OR ;
\\  ok  \

: LEAP?  ( year -- )
    DUP .
    LEAP IF ." is" ELSE  ." isn't" THEN  ."  a leap
year." ;
\\  ok  \

2000 LEAP?
\\  2000 is a leap year. ok     \

2001  LEAP?
\\  2001 isn't a leap year. ok  \

2002  LEAP?
\\  2002 isn't a leap year. ok  \
```

```
2003  LEAP?
\\  2003 isn't a leap year. ok  \


2004  LEAP?
\\  2004 is a leap year. ok      \
```

\ One word can be saved by deciding if a year isn't a
\ leap year

```
: -LEAP  ( year -- flag )
\ nonzero flag means not a leap year
    DUP 100 MOD 0=  OVER 400 MOD AND  SWAP 4 MOD OR ;
\\  ok  \
```

\ Using EXIT skips some tests for most years

```
: LEAPX  ( year -- flag )
    DUP 4 MOD IF DROP FALSE EXIT THEN
    DUP 100 MOD SWAP 400 MOD 0= OR ;
\\  ok  \

: -LEAPX  ( year -- flag )
    DUP 4 MOD IF EXIT THEN
    DUP 100 MOD 0= SWAP 400 MOD AND ;
\\  ok  \
```

Forth's other bit operators are:

INVERT (x1 -- x2) toggles bits of *x1*

2*   (x1 -- x2) shifts bits of *x1* one place left, leaving the least
significant bit zero. Like multiply by 2.
A fast 2 * on most systems.
(0000 1111 -> 0001 1110)

2/   (x1 -- x2) shifts bits of *x1* one place right, leaving the most
significant bit unchanged. (could be the sign bit)
A fast 2 / on most systems.
(1000 1111 -> 1100 0111)

LSHIFT (x1 u -- x2) shifts bits of *x1 u* places to the left,
putting zeros in the empty places on the right.
(0000 1111 -> 0001 1110)

RSHIFT (x1 u -- x2) shifts bits of *x1 u* places to the right, putting
zeroes in the into empty places on the left.
(1000 1111 ->0100 0111)

Try:

```
0 DUP B. INVERT B.
\\  0 11111111111111111111111111111111  ok  \

1 DUP B. INVERT B.
\\  1 11111111111111111111111111111110  ok  \

-1 DUP B. INVERT B.
\\  11111111111111111111111111111111 0  ok  \

1 DUP B. 2* DUP B. .
\\  1 10 2  ok      \

-1 DUP B. 2* DUP B. .
\\  11111111111111111111111111111111
\\  11111111111111111111111111111110  ok-1 \

2 DUP B. 2/ DUP B. .     \\  10 1 1  ok-1  \
-2 DUP B. 2/ DUP B. .
\\  11111111111111111111111111111110
\\  11111111111111111111111111111111 -1  ok \

1 DUP B. 4 LSHIFT DUP B. .
\\  1 10000 16  ok        \

1 DUP B. 8 LSHIFT DUP B. .
\\  1 100000000 256  ok  \

-1 DUP B. 4 LSHIFT DUP B. .
\\  11111111111111111111111111111111
\\  11111111111111111111111111110000 -16  ok \

-1 DUP B. 8 LSHIFT DUP B. .
\\  11111111111111111111111111111111
\\  11111111111111111111111100000000 -256  ok

\ 2 to the nth power
: 2^  ( +n -- u )  1 SWAP LSHIFT ;
\\  ok  \

0 2^ U.   \\   1  ok  \

1 2^ U.   \\   2  ok  \

2 2^ U.   \\   4  ok  \

3 2^ U.   \\   8  ok  \

4 2^ U.   \\   16  ok  \

10 2^ U.  \\ 1024  ok  \
```

```
-1 DUP B. 4 RSHIFT DUP B. .
\\   111111111111111111111111111111111
\\   11111111111111111111111111111 268435455  ok

-1 DUP B. 8 RSHIFT DUP B. .
\\   1111111111111111111111111111111111
\\   111111111111111111111111 16 777 215  ok  \
```

The following code uses several bit operators. It assumes, that you have saved lightsVFX.f into the C:\FORTH_LITE folder

```
A-------------------------------------------------------------
\ lightsVFX.f                              \\
\ Usage: INCLUDE C:\FORTH_LITE\lightsVFX.f  \\
\ or to try just copy the code from
\ lightsVFX.f  uses to
\ : BRIGHT  ( -- )  TRUE LIGHTS !  LAMP ;
\ into VFX, then enter BRIGHT to start the Word
\ lightsVFX.f, uses CRS and SPACES
\instead of AT-XY for formatting

VARIABLE LIGHTS
\ Set nth bit only

: MASK   ( n1 -- n2 ) 1 SWAP LSHIFT ;

: ON? ( n1 -- n2|0 ) MASK LIGHTS @ AND ;

: LIGHT   ( -- )   ." @ " ;

: .LIGHT?   ( u -- )   ON? IF LIGHT ELSE 3 SPACES THEN ;

: SPACES ( u -- ) 0 ?DO SPACE LOOP ;

: CRS   ( u -- ) 0 ?DO CR LOOP ;


: LAMP  ( -- )   PAGE
   4 CRS 26 SPACES   ." LIGHTS"

   2 CRS 5 SPACES 0 16 0 ?DO  DUP .LIGHT?  1+  LOOP
DROP

   CR  4 SPACES  0 16 0 ?DO  DUP 3 .R  1+  LOOP  DROP

   CR CR  80 SPACES

   2 CRS 13 SPACES  ." n ON/OFF/TOGGLE /
BRIGHT/DARK/BYE " ;


\ Set individual lights
```

```
: ON   ( u -- )  MASK LIGHTS @ OR LIGHTS ! LAMP ;

: OFF ( u -- ) MASK INVERT LIGHTS @ AND LIGHTS ! LAMP
;

: TOGGLE ( u -- )   MASK LIGHTS @ XOR LIGHTS !  LAMP ;
\ Set all lights
: DARK   ( -- )   FALSE LIGHTS !  LAMP ;

: BRIGHT   ( -- )   TRUE LIGHTS !  LAMP ;

BRIGHT

A----------------------------------------------------------------------------------------
```

Cut and paste the code between A---- and A---- into VFX first

And VFX will come up with:

```
\\                          LIGHTS
\\
\\      @  @  @  @  @  @  @  @  @  @  @  @  @  @  @  @
\\      0  1  2  3  4  5  6  7  8  9 10 11 12 13 14 15
\\
\\              n ON/OFF/TOGGLE / BRIGHT/DARK/BYE   ok
```

Use the commands n - on/off/toggle, all on, all off or BYE

```
0 OFF
\ from now on only the 2 main lines are shown
\\         @  @  @  @  @  @  @  @  @  @  @  @  @  @  @
\\      0  1  2  3  4  5  6  7  8  9 10 11 12 13 14 15

1 OFF
\\         @  @  @  @  @  @  @  @  @  @  @  @  @  @  @
\\      0  1  2  3  4  5  6  7  8  9 10 11 12 13 14 15

2 OFF
\\            @  @  @  @  @  @  @  @  @  @  @  @  @  @
\\      0  1  2  3  4  5  6  7  8  9 10 11 12 13 14 15

3 OFF
\\               @  @  @  @  @  @  @  @  @  @  @  @  @
\\      0  1  2  3  4  5  6  7  8  9 10 11 12 13 14 15

0 ON
\\      @        @  @  @  @  @  @  @  @  @  @  @  @  @
\\      0  1  2  3  4  5  6  7  8  9 10 11 12 13 14 15
```

1 ON
```
\\        @  @     @  @  @  @  @  @  @  @  @  @  @  @  @
\\        0  1  2  3  4  5  6  7  8  9 10 11 12 13 14 15
```

2 ON
```
\\        @  @  @  @  @  @  @  @  @  @  @  @  @  @  @  @
\\        0  1  2  3  4  5  6  7  8  9 10 11 12 13 14 15
```

DARK
```
\\
\\        0  1  2  3  4  5  6  7  8  9 10 11 12 13 14 15
```

BRIGHT
```
\\        @  @  @  @  @  @  @  @  @  @  @  @  @  @  @  @
\\        0  1  2  3  4  5  6  7  8  9 10 11 12 13 14 15
```

BYE
```
\\            \  exits VFX
```

Now restart VFX and save the code as file into C:\FORTH_LITE as you have done with other programs before.

Then load and start executing the file from this folder

INCLUDE C:\FORTH_LITE\lightsVFX.f

```
\\                              LIGHTS
\\
\\        @  @  @  @  @  @  @  @  @  @  @  @  @  @  @  @
\\        0  1  2  3  4  5  6  7  8  9 10 11 12 13 14 15
\\
\\
\\
\\            n ON/OFF/TOGGLE / BRIGHT/DARK/BYE   ok
```

BYE

Lesson 27 - *A Software Stack*

Words in this lesson: 2@   2!

For an excursion, here are some words for extra software stacks you might need.

Each stack element occupies a cell; stack depth is checked. To create a stack, specify its maximum depth and its name.

The name is used when PUSHing, POPing, displaying, and EMPTYing.

For an implementation of stacks with elements of arbitrary size, see Len Zettel's <u>User Stacks in Forth</u> (not there anymore so you have to search). And for a use of such user stacks see Len's <u>Discrete Event Simulation in Forth</u> (not there anymore so you have to search).

First, two words to add to your repertory:

```
2!  ( x1 x2 addr -- ) does SWAP OVER ! CELL+ !
                          \ explanation of the word 2!

2@  ( addr -- x1 x2 ) does DUP CELL+ @ SWAP @
                          \ explanation of the word 2@
```

2! and 2@ are typically used to store and fetch "double numbers", which are integers 2 cells wide.

In our software-stack implementation, we'll use 2@ to fetch values from the two addresses starting at addr.

Try:

```
A-------------------------------------------------------------
\ Software stack implementation
\ Two additional words
: ++   ( addr -- )    1 SWAP +! ;

: --   ( addr -- )   -1 SWAP +! ; \\

\ Fetch from address and advance address
: @+  ( addr -- addr+ x )  DUP CELL+ SWAP @ ;  \\

\ Make a stack that is u cells deep
\ Usage:   u STACK <name>
: STACK   ( u -- )
   CREATE          \ stack <name>
```

```
0 ,                \ initialize depth
DUP ,              \ set maximum depth
CELLS ALLOT ;   \ reserve space
```

```
\ If there's room on stack, move x from the
\ Forth stack to it else leave x on the Forth stack
: PUSH  ( x stack -- |x )
  DUP 2@ >
  IF  DUP ++  @+ CELLS + !
  ELSE  DROP ." Stack full"  THEN ;
```

```
\ If there is an x, move it from stack to the Forth
\ stack, else put nothing on the Forth stack
: POP  ( stack -- x| )
  DUP @+ ?DUP
  IF  ROT --  CELLS + @
  ELSE  DROP ." Empty stack"  THEN ;
```

```
\ Display stack items, bottom --> top
: .STACK  ( stack -- )
  @+ ?DUP
  IF 0 ?DO  CELL+  DUP ?  LOOP
  ELSE  ." Empty stack"  THEN
  DROP ;
```

```
\ Clear stack
: EMPTY  ( stack -- )  0 SWAP ! ;
```

A--

Try examples

3 STACK MYSTACK
\\ MYSTACK is redefined   ok

33 MYSTACK PUSH
\\ ok

-33 MYSTACK PUSH
\\ ok

MYSTACK .STACK
\\ 33 -33   ok

MYSTACK POP .
\\ -33 ok

MYSTACK POP .
\\ 33 ok

76 MYSTACK PUSH

99 MYSTACK PUSH

MYSTACK .STACK
\\ 76 99 ok

MYSTACK EMPTY
\\ ok

MYSTACK .STACK
\\ Empty stack ok

<u>**BYE**</u>

Lesson 28 - *Characters A*

Words in this lesson: EMIT   CHAR   BL

Characters, like other data in a computer, are bit patterns treated by Forth in a particular way. An integer and a character can have the same bit pattern.

EMIT (char --) displays a character

CHAR (-- char) puts the next character on the stack.

BL (-- char) puts the value for space (blank -decimal 32) on the stack.

Try:

BL DUP . EMIT
```
\\  32  ok
\  BL on stack, another BL as duplicated
\  on stack, send 32, then SPACE
```

BL DUP EMIT .
```
\\  32  ok
\  BL on stack, another BL on
\  stack, send SPACE, then 32
```

65 DUP . EMIT
```
\\ 65 A ok
\  65 on stack, another 65 on
\  stack, send 65, then as ASCII A
```

CHAR A DUP . EMIT
```
\\ 65 A ok
\  Char A onto stack, DUP,
\  send 65, send A
```

Decimal 65 is the ASCII (American Standard Code for Information Interchange) and ISO IRV (International Standards Organization/ International Reverence Version) code for 'A'.

Both standards have the same character interpretation for codes 32-126 except for 36.

Try:

36 EMIT
```
\\  $ ok
\   send the $ sign
```

If a $ is displayed, it's ASCII. In VFX it is ASCII.

Codes 0-31 are control codes with generally accepted meanings. Codes beyond 126 exist in other standards.

We will stick to 32-126. Here are characters 32-126 with the implementation-defined character 127 thrown in.

Try:

```
\ Display next n characters and their codes
: .CHARS ( c n -- c+n )
   0 ?DO  DUP 5 .R  DUP SPACE EMIT  1+  LOOP ;
\\ ok  \
```

20 5 .chars
```
\\ 20 _  21 _  22 _  23 _  24 _ ok-3
```

```
\ Display characters 32-127 and their codes
: .CHARS32-127 ( -- )
   BL 12 0 ?DO  CR 8 .CHARS  LOOP  DROP ;
\\ ok  \
```

.CHARS32-127
```
\\     32      33 !   34 "   35 #   36 $   37 %   38 &   39 '
\\     40 (    41 )   42 *   43 +   44 ,   45 -   46 .   47 /
\\     48 0    49 1   50 2   51 3   52 4   53 5   54 6   55 7
\\     56 8    57 9   58 :   59 ;   60 <   61 =   62 >   63 ?
\\     64 @    65 A   66 B   67 C   68 D   69 E   70 F   71 G
\\     72 H    73 I   74 J   75 K   76 L   77 M   78 N   79 O
\\     80 P    81 Q   82 R   83 S   84 T   85 U   86 V   87 W
\\     88 X    89 Y   90 Z   91 [   92 \   93 ]   94 ^   95 _
\\     96 `    97 a   98 b   99 c  100 d  101 e  102 f  103 g
\\    104 h   105 i  106 j  107 k  108 l  109 m  110 n  111 o
\\    112 p   113 q  114 r  115 s  116 t  117 u  118 v  119 w
\\    120 x   121 y  122 z  123 {  124 |  125 }  126 ~  127 ▯
\\  ok  \
```

BYE

Lesson 29 - *Characters B*

Words in this lesson: [CHAR]   KEY

To put a particular character in a definition, use [CHAR].
To wait for a character from the keyboard, use KEY.

[CHAR] <char>   in a definition puts char on the stack when the
definition is executed.

KEY (-- char) waits for a key press, then puts the character pressed
on the stack.

Try:

```
\ Is character Y or y?
: Y?  ( char -- flag )
   DUP [CHAR] Y =  SWAP [CHAR] y = OR ;
\\   ok  \

: YES?  ( -- )
   ." Press Y for yes."  KEY
   Y? IF  ." Yes"  ELSE  ." No"  THEN ;
\\   ok  \

YES?            \
\  Press Y for yes.
\\ Y
\\ Yes ok   \

\ KEY does not automatically EMIT to the screen
: PRESS  ( -- )
   ." Please press a key. " KEY
   ." You pressed " EMIT ;

PRESS
\\  Please press a key.   \\  x
\\ You pressed x ok  \
```

Homework: rewrite PRESS, so it stays in a loop and only exits when you
type x or X

BYE

Lesson 30 *Characters C*

Words in this lesson: C   C,   C@   C!   **CHARS**
CHAR+   ALIGN

C, C@ C! CHARS CHAR+ are character versions of the
, @ ! CELLS CELL+ words you know already.

Although on the stack a character occupies a cell, in many Forths a
character in memory occupies less space than a cell. Character codes 0-
127 fit into 7 bits, and 8 bits (a byte) can hold codes 0-255.

A Forth with 8-bit characters can therefore store two characters in 16 bits
and 4 characters in 32 bits.

Since , @ ! CELLS CELL+ are intended for cell-size values in memory,
character versions are need for character-size values.

C,	(char	--	)	reserves a character of memory and stores character-size value in it.
C@	(c-addr	-- char	)	fetches char from c-addr.
C!	(char	c-addr --	)	stores char at c-addr.
CHARS	(n1	-- n2	)	n1 chars fit into n2 address units.
CHAR+	(c-addr1	-- c-addr2)		advances c-addr1 by one character.

ALIGN assures proper placement of cell values. Use after C, and CHARS
ALLOT.

Try:

```
CREATE CHARACTER  CHAR A C, CHAR  B C, ALIGN
\\ ok     \

CHARACTER C@ EMIT
\\  A ok  \

CHARACTER CHAR+ C@ EMIT
\\  B ok  \

CHAR Z CHARACTER C!
\\  ok    \
```

```
CHAR ! CHARACTER CHAR+ C!
\\  ok   \


CHARACTER C@ EMIT
\\  Z ok  \

CHARACTER CHAR+ C@ EMIT
\\  ! ok  \

: C!+  ( c-addr char -- c-addr+ )  OVER C! CHAR+ ;
   \\ ok       \

    \ C@+ and EMITS we'll meet again as COUNT and TYPE

: C@+  ( c-addr -- c-addr+ char )  DUP CHAR+ SWAP C@ ;
   \\ ok       \

: EMITS  ( c-addr n )  0 MAX  0 ?DO  C@+ EMIT  LOOP
DROP ;
\\ ok        \

CREATE 5CHARS 5 CHARS ALLOT ALIGN
\\ 5CHARS is redefined  ok \

5CHARS
\\ ok-1        \

CHAR F C!+  CHAR o C!+  CHAR r C!+  CHAR t C!+  CHAR h
C!+
\\ ok-1       \

DROP
\ drop the c-addr remaining after the last C!+
\\ ok        \

5CHARS 5 EMITS
\\ Forth ok \


BYE
```

Lesson 31 - *Strings Part 1*

Words in this lesson: `S"` `TYPE`

A string is an array of characters. We already used `."` and `.(` to display strings. To just define a string one can use:

`S" ` *text*`"` (`-- a u`), is used in a definition, compiles *text* up to but not including the next `"`,
and returns the character address *c-addr* and the length of the string *u* when the definition is executed.
Using `S"` in a definition is an easy way to create a string constant.

Try:

```
: HI  S" Ni hao!" ;
\\  ok  \
```

```
HI CHARS DUMP
\\ 004C:BC36   4E 69 20 68 61 6F 21 00
\\  00 00 C3 04 64 75 6D 70  Ni hao!...
\\  C.dump ok-3
```

If your ANS Forth system has file words, `S"` can also be used outside a definition to put *text* in a temporary buffer that could be overwritten by the next use of `S"` outside a definition.

This `S"` also returns an address and a length. I'll assume that you can use `S"` outside a definition.

Try:

```
S" Xiexie."  .S CHARS DUMP
```

```
S" Bu keqi." .S CHARS DUMP
   \\   004C:9966   4E 69 20 68 61 6F 21 00   00 00 C3 04
44 55
   \\   4D 50  Ni hao!...C.DUMP  \
   \\    ok  \
```

`TYPE` (`c-addr u --`) displays the first *u* characters of a string, starting at address *c-addr*.

Try:

```
\ Assumes HI is defined
```

```
HI TYPE
\\  Ni hao! Ok  \
```

```
\ Equivalent to : GOODBYE  ." Zaijian" ;
: GOOD-BYE  S" Zaijian" TYPE ;
\\  ok  \
```

GOOD-BYE
```
\\  Zaijian ok  \
```


BYE

Lesson 32 - *Strings Part 2*

Words in this lesson: COUNT   MOVE

Since most string functions use the starting address of a string and the string's length, it's convenient to store the length along with the string.

In Forth, a string that has its length in a character-sized address and the string itself in the following character addresses is called a *counted string*.

For example, the counted string "Leo" is: 3 'L' 'e' 'o'. The word that takes the address of a counted string and returns the address and length of the string is:

COUNT (c-addr1 -- c-addr2 u) returns the address *c-addr2* of the first character and the number of characters *u* in the counted string at *c-addr1*.

COUNT is effectively **DUP CHAR+ SWAP** C@. It is used for other things besides getting the start and "count" of a counted string and would have been better named C@+.

Since the "count" is stored in a character-sized space, the maximum length of a counted string can't be larger than the largest number that space can hold. For a Forth with 8-bit characters, the maximum length of a counted string is 255. However, longer strings are easy to accommodate in Forth.

The easiest way to create a counted string is to MOVE a string (c-addr u) into data space.

MOVE (addr1 u addr2 --) copies the contents of *u* consecutive
address units at *addr1* to the
u consecutive address units at *addr2*.

Since MOVE uses address units, it can be used for any type of data. The two Forth words **CMOVE** and **CMOVE>** specifically copy characters, but we will just use **MOVE** and specify that we are moving CHARS.

I am getting tired of typing addr c-addr char in comments, so from now on and to shorten it, I will just write   a ca c.
Also, I will try to get more organized and clear with the words,
continue to write ANS Forth words in uppercase,
but start writing non-ANS Forth words in lowercase so we can distinguish them.

Try:

```
CREATE my-string   50 CHARS ALLOT
\\   ok    \
```

```
\ Copy ca1 u as a counted string to ca2
: place  ( ca1 u ca2 -- )
\\   PLACE is redefined  \
```

```
2DUP 2>R   CHAR+ SWAP CHARS MOVE   2R> C! ;
\\   ok    \
```

```
S" The quick brown fox jumped over the lazy dog."
\\   ok-2 \
```

```
my-string COUNT TYPE
\\ The quick brown fox jumped
\\ over the lazy dog. Ok  \
```

```
\ Illustrating COUNT as C@+
: my-type  ( ca u -- )  0 ?DO COUNT EMIT LOOP DROP ;
\\   ok    \
```

```
my-string COUNT my-type
\\ The quick brown fox jumped over the lazy dog. Ok   \
```

BYE

Lesson 33 - *Strings Part 3*

Words in this lesson: `/TRAILING` `FILL` `BLANK` `-TRAILING`

A penknife for strings is:

`/STRING` (ca1 u1 n -- ca2 u2) returns *ca2* = ca1+nchars, *u2* = u1-n.
`/STRING` is officially called "slash string"; a nicer name would be "cut string".

`/STRING` could be defined:

```
: /STRING ( ca1 u1 n -- ca2 us ) TUCK - >R CHARS + R> ;
```

Try:

```
\ Three other words useful in string processing.
\ Skip leading c's in ca u;
\ return remaining
\ string ca' u'
: skip  ( ca u c -- ca' u' )
\\   SKIP is redefined  \
   >R
   BEGIN DUP WHILE OVER C@ R@ = WHILE 1
     /STRING REPEAT   THEN
        R> DROP ;
\\  ok  \
```

```
\ Look for 1st c in ca u; return ca' u' including c

: scan  ( ca u c -- ca' u' )
\\   SCAN is redefined  \

   >R
   BEGIN DUP WHILE OVER C@ R@ <> WHILE 1 /STRING REPEAT
THEN
   R> DROP ;
\\  ok  \
```

```
\ From ca u, return 1st "word" ca2 u2 and remainder ca1
\ u1 WORD is a Forth word, so I'll call this:
: "word"  ( ca u -- ca1 u1 ca2 u2 )
   BL skip  2DUP 2>R  BL scan  DUP 2R> ROT - ;
\\ ok  \
```

```
\ Illustration using word
: list-words  ( ca u -- )
```

```
    BEGIN DUP WHILE "word" CR TYPE REPEAT 2DROP ;
\\  ok  \
```

```
S" To be or not to be" list-words
\\  To   \
\\  be   \
\\  or   \
\\  not  \
\\  to   \
\\  be   \
\\  ok   \
```

FILL BLANK and -TRAILING are also handy.

FILL (ca u c --) stores *c* in *u* consecutive characters of memory
beginning at *ca.*

```
: FILL ( ca u c -- ) ROT ROT 0 ?DO 2DUP C! CHAR+ LOOP
2DROP ;
\\ FILL is redefined  ok \
```

BLANK (ca u --) FILLs with spaces.
```
: BLANK ( ca u -- ) BL FILL ;
\\ BLANK is redefined  ok \
```

-TRAILING (ca u1 -- ca u2) returns *ca u1* minus any trailing
spaces. "Dash trailing" Gets rid of any spaces at the end.

```
: <skip  ( ca u1 c -- ca u2 )
   >R
   BEGIN DUP WHILE 1- 2DUP CHARS + C@ R@ <> UNTIL 1+
THEN
   R> DROP ;
\\    ok  \
```

```
: -TRAILING  ( ca u1 -- ca u2 >  BL <skip ;
\\  -TRAILING is redefined  \
```

Try:

```
CREATE BUFFER 40 CHARS ALLOT
\\  ok  \
```

```
BUFFER 40 CHAR Y FILL
\\  ok  \
```

```
BUFFER 40 TYPE
\\   YYYYYYYYYYYYYYYYYYYYYYYYYYYYYYYYYYYYYYYY ok  \
```

Now

```
BUFFER 20 CHARS + 20 BLANK
\\  ok  \
```

```
BUFFER 40 TYPE
\\  YYYYYYYYYYYYYYYYYYYY                    ok   \
```

```
BUFFER 40 -TRAILING TYPE
\\  YYYYYYYYYYYYYYYYYYYY ok \
\  Spaces cut off
```

```
BUFFER 20 BLANK
\\  ok \
```

```
BUFFER 40 TYPE
\\  ok \
```

```
BUFFER 40 -TRAILING TYPE
\\  ok  \
\ all spaces cut out
```

You can see the results a lot better when you copy the lines, paste and execute them in VFX, one directly after the other.

BYE

Lesson 34 - *Strings Part 4*

Words in this lesson: SEARCH COMPARE

String searches and compares are done with SEARCH and COMPARE:

SEARCH (ca1 u1 ca2 u2 -- ca3|ca1 u3|u1 true|false)
searches *ca1 u1* for the string specified by *ca2 u2*.
If found, returns address *ca3* of first match, characters remaining *u3*, and
true, else returns *ca1 u1 false*.

COMPARE (ca1 u1 ca2 u2 -- -1|0|1) compares *ca1 u1* and *ca2*
u2 and returns *-1* if *ca1 u1* is less than *ca2 u2*, *0* if the two strings are the
same, and *1* if *ca1 u1* is greater than *ca2 u2*. (See the examples for what is
meant by less, same, and greater.)

Remember: **SEARCH and COMPARE are case sensitive.**

Try:

```
: s1   S" Out out out!" ;
\\   ok   \
```

```
\ define a string consisting of
\ the 3 different words Out out out!
\ if we put b for the space for visibility
\ the string looks like Outboutbout!
```

```
s1 s" Out" SEARCH . TYPE
\\   -1 Out out out! ok   \
```

```
s1 S" out" SEARCH . TYPE
\\   -1 out out! ok        \
```

```
s1 s" out!" SEARCH . TYPE
\\ -1 out! ok              \
```

```
s1 S" OUT"   SEARCH . TYPE
\\   0 Out out out! ok   \
```

```
\ Char is lowercase?
: lower?  ( c -- t|f)   [CHAR] a - 26 U< ;
\\   ok   \
```

```
\ Make char uppercase
: upper  ( c -- c' )   DUP lower? BL AND XOR ;
\\   UPPER is redefined   ok   \
```

```
\ Make string uppercase
: supper  ( a u -- )
```

```
    0 ?DO DUP C@ upper OVER C! CHAR+ LOOP DROP ;
\\   ok   \


s1 2DUP supper S" ouT" 2DUP supper SEARCH . TYPE
\\   -1 OUT OUT OUT! Ok \
\ changed to upper case \
: outs?  ( a u -- n )
   2DUP supper  0 >R
   BEGIN S" OUT" SEARCH
   WHILE R> 1+ >R  1 /STRING
   REPEAT  2DROP
   R> ;
\\   ok       \
```

Now let us define another string to work on:

```
S" out spout mouth" outs? .
\\   3  ok   \

: ABC?  S" ABC" COMPARE . ;
\\   ok       \

S" ABC" ABC?
\\  0  ok  \

S" abc" ABC?
\\  1  ok  \

S" AB" ABC?
\\ -1  ok  \

S" ABCD" ABC?
\\  1  ok  \

S" B" ABC?
\\  1  ok  \

S" @ABC" ABC?
\\ -1  ok  \

S" abc" 2DUP supper ABC?
\\  0  ok  \

\ Compare for integers
: sgn  ( n - -1|0|1 )
   -1 MAX 1 MIN ;
\\  ok  \

: ncompare  ( n1 n2 -- -1|0|1 )
   - sgn ;
\\  ok  \
```

```
-10 sgn .
\\  -1  ok  \

0 sgn .
\\   0  ok  \

10 sgn .
\\   1  ok  \

10 5 ncompare .
\\   1  ok  \

5 5 ncompare .
\\   0  ok  \

-10 5 ncompare .
\\  -1  ok  \
```

BYE

Lesson 35 - *Values*

Words in this lesson: VALUE TO

In some programs a value is set once or infrequently and used often.

For example, many words that have to do with files require a file identifier (fid) that is returned when the file is created or opened. The fid could easily be stored in a variable:

VARIABLE fid
\\   ok
\and fetched whenever needed \

fid
\\   ok-1 \

Many Forths provide a cross between a constant and the variable that is called a value. It might be used as follows:

0 VALUE fid
\\   FID is redefined   ok-1
\ Take 0 and this as the value of the variable fid

10   TO fid
\\   ok   \ Set fid to 10

. . .

fid (-- u) .
\\   10 ok \ Returns u

x **VALUE** *name* defines the word *name* that returns *x* unless the value to be returned is changed by TO.

y TO name makes then *name* return *y*.

y +TO name, available in some Forths, increments by *y* the value returned by *name*.

Try:

FALSE VALUE love
\\   ok \

LOVE .
\\ 0 ok \

love FALSE = .
\\   ok-1   \

```
love  .
\\ 0  ok-1 \

love love = TO love
\\   ok-1       \

love  .
\\  -1  ok-1  \

love TRUE = .
\\  -1  ok-1  \
```

BYE

Lesson 36 – *Locals*

Words in this lesson: LOCALS | TO

A named VARIABLE or VALUE can appear in several parts of a program: its possible use is "global" within the program, meaning the same variable unique and used everywhere in the program.

Forths that implement "locals" also provide for value names that apply only within the word they are defined in. So the same name can be used in different words with different values each time.

Using locals can prevent the bug in which a change in a variable in one part of the program has unintended consequences in another part.

Locals can also make a definition easier to write and to read by making values explicit and reducing stack manipulation. Here are definitions of vswap without and with locals.

This is good to know, but more in the advanced area, only go there if you need to:

```
\ Exchange values of two variables
\ Without locals
: vswap1  ( addr1 addr2 -- )   2DUP 2>R  @ SWAP @  R> !
R> ! ;
\\  ok-1  \
```

```
\ Exchange values of two variables
\ With locals
: vswap2  ( addr1 addr2 -- )
    LOCALS| v1 v2 |
    v1 @ v2 @ v1 ! v2 ! ;
\\  ok-1  \
```

LOCALS | allows the creation of up to eight (in some Forths more than eight) names as local identifiers. The list of names ends with |.
Given 0 1 LOCALS| a b |, a returns 1 and b returns 0.
(And some Forths implement a word that allows the values and the names to be placed in the same order.)

y TO *name* makes *name* return *y*. The usage is the same as that for VALUEs.

y +TO *name*, available in some Forths, increments by *y* the value returned by *name*. Again, the usage is the same as that for VALUEs.

I wrote the following after trying to explain how to find out if a given integer is a prime number.

A--

```
\ prime.f LW 10 Jan 02002+ Leo Wong
\ An integer is a prime number if it can be evenly
\ divided
\ only by itself and 1.
\ Integers that are not prime numbers are composite
\ numbers, divisible without a remainder by
\ numbers (factors) other than itself and 1.
\ We want to find out if a given integer n is prime or
\ composite.
\ Two English words for easier reading code.
: not  ( ? -- ? )  0= ;
\\ NOT is redefined  ok-1 \

: between  ( n1 n2 n3 -- ? )  1+ WITHIN ;
\\ BETWEEN is redefined  ok-1 \

\ If n is evenly divisible by f,
\ then f is a factor of n.

\ Is f a factor of n?
: factor  ( n f -- ? )  MOD 0= ;
\\ FACTOR is redefined  ok-1  \

\ 2 is a factor of even numbers.
: even  ( n -- ? )  2 factor ;
\\ EVEN is redefined  ok-1     \

\ A composite number has at least one factor less than
\ or equal to its square root, so we only try f's whose
\ squares are less than or equal to n.

: square  ( f -- f*f )  DUP * ;
\\ SQUARE is redefined  ok-1  \

\ Find out if n has a factor between 3 and its
\ square root

: factorable  ( n -- ? )

    3 LOCALS| f n |
\ Start with f = 3     \

    BEGIN

    n f factor not WHILE
\ Continue if f not \
\ a factor of
```

```
    f 2 + TO f
\ make f the next odd number \

    n f square < not WHILE
\ Continue if f squared <= n \

  REPEAT THEN

    n f factor ;
\\  ok-1   \

: prime?  ( +n -- )
   LOCALS| n |
   n 1 3 between IF ." prime"        \ 1, 2, 3 : prime
   ELSE n even IF  ." composite " \ Even & > 2 :
                                   \ composite
   ELSE n factorable IF ." composite"  ELSE ." prime"
THEN
   THEN THEN ;
\\    ok-1   \
```

A--

Copy the code between A---- and A---- into VFX and try:

2 prime?   \\   prime   ok \

8 prime?   \\   composite ok \

11 prime?   \\   prime ok

4766 prime? \\   composite   ok \

A third example of using locals multiplies complex numbers. To understand what happens is not for the faint hearted:

```
\ complex multiply by ward mcfarland
: ComplexMultiply ( x1\y1\x2\y2 -- xp\yp )
\ calculate (x1 + j*y1) * (x2 + j*y2)
\             = (x1*x2 - y1*y2) + j (x1*y2 + x2*y1)
   locals| y2 x2 y1 x1 |
   x1 x2 *
   y1 y2 *   -
   x1 y2 *
   x2 y1 *   +
;
\\  ok  \
```

Without locals a solution might be:

```
: cm  2OVER 2OVER ROT ROT * >R * >R ROT * >R * R> - 2R>
+ ;
\\  ok  \
```

[To be continued....]

This is the end of the first tutorial, using the PC only, the one on using external hardware will follow

BYE

\ #### \

Appendix

Forth LITE words sorted alphabetically

ASCII character set table

SEE .S - what VFX Forth sends back

MSP430 and hardware

FORTH LITE WORDS

Word	Stack Activity	Description
-	n1/u1 n2/u2 -- n3/u3	subtract n1-n2
!	x a-addr --	store cell in memory
(	--	skip input until)
*	n1 n2 -- n3	signed multiply
*/	n1 n2 n3 -- n4	n1*n2/n3
*/MOD	n1 n2 n3 -- n4 n5	n1*n2/n3, rem&quot
.	n --	display n signed
."	--	compile string to print
.R	n1 n2 --	display n1 right aligned in a field n2 char. wide field
.S	--	print stack contents
/	n1 n2 -- n3	signed divide
/MOD	n1 n2 -- n3 n4	signed divide/rem'dr
/STRING	a u n -- a+n u-n	trim string
:	--	begin a colon definition
;	--	end a colon definition
?	a-addr --	display value stored at a-addr.
?DO	n1 n2 -- R: -- loop-sys	if n1 is equal to n2, continue execution after LOOP.
?DUP	x -- 0 | x x	DUP if nonzero
@	a-addr -- x	fetch cell from memory
[CHAR]	--	compile character literal

\	--	backslash
+	n1/u1 n2/u2 -- n3/u3	add n1+n2
+!	n/u a-addr --	add cell to memory
+LOOP	adrs -- L: 0 a1 a2 .. aN --	finish a loop
<	n1 n2 -- flag	test n1<n2, signed
<R	-- x R: x --	move x return stack to data stack.
=	x1 x2 -- flag	true if x1 is bit-for-bit x2.
>	n1 n2 -- flag	test n1>n2, signed
>R	x -- R: -- x	push to return stack
0<	n --	flag true if TOS negative
0<>	x -- flag	flag true if x is not equal to zero
0=	n/u -- flag	return true if TOS=0
1-	n1/u1 -- n2/u2	subtract 1 from TOS
1+	n1/u1 -- n2/u2	add 1 to TOS
2!	x1 x2 a-addr --	store 2 cells
2*	x1 -- x2	arithmetic left shift
2/	x1 -- x2	arithmetic right shift
2@	a-addr -- x1 x2	fetch 2 cells
2>R	x1 x2 -- R: -- x1 x2	transfer cell pair to return stack
2DROP	x1 x2 --	drop 2 cells
2DUP	x1 x2 -- x1 x2 x1 x2	dup top 2 cells
2OVER	x1 x2 x3 x4 -- x1 x2 x3 x4 x1 x2	see stack activity, x1 x2 over
2R@	- - x1 x2 R: x1 x2 - - x1 x2	copy cell pair from R to D satck
2R>	-- x1 x2 R: x1 x2 --	transfer cell pair x1 x2 from the return stack
2SWAP	x1 x2 x3 x4 -- x3 x4 x1 x2	per diagram
ABS	n1 -- +n2	absolute value
AGAIN	adrs --	uncond'l backward branch
ALIGN	--	align HERE
ALLOT	n --	allocate n bytes in dict
AND	x1 x2 -- x3	logical AND
AT-XY	x y --	send esc-sequence to terminal
BASE	-- a-addr	holds conversion radix

BEGIN	-- adrs	target for bwd. branch
BL	--	char, an ASCII space
BLANK	c-addr u --	store space in u consecutive characters beginning at c-addr.
C!	char c-addr --	store char in memory
C,	char --	append char to dict
C@	c-addr -- char	fetch char from memory
CELLS	n1 -- n2	cells->adrs units
CELL+	a-addr1 -- a-addr2	
CHAR	-- char	parse ASCII character
CHAR+	c-addr1 -- c-addr2	add char size
CHARS	n1 -- n2	chars->adrs units
COMPARE	c-addr1 u1 c-addr2 u2 -- n	
CONSTANT	--	define a Forth constant
COUNT	c-addr1 -- c-addr2 u	counted->adr/len
CR	--	output new line
CREATE	--	create an empty definition
DECIMAL	--	set number base to decimal
DEPTH	-- +n	number of items on stack
DO	-- adrs L: -- 0	start a loop
DROP	x --	drop top of stack
DUMP	adr n --	dump memory
DUP	x -- x x	duplicate top of stack
ELSE	adrs1 -- adrs2	branch for IF..ELSE
EMIT	c --	output character to console
ERASE	addr u --	clear all bits in all u units of memory beginning at addr.
EXIT	--	exit a colon definition
FALSE	0	return a false flag.
FILL	c-addr u char --	fill memory with char
HERE	-- addr	returns dictionary ptr
HEX	--	set number base to hex
I	-- n R: sys1 sys2 -- sys1 sys2	get the innermost loop index

IF	-- adrs	conditional forward branch
INCLUDED	c-addr u --	open the file specified by c-addr u and interpret it.
INVERT	x1 -- x2	bitwise inversion
J	-- n R: 4*sys -- 4*sys	get the second loop index
KEY	-- c	get character from keyboard
LEAVE	-- L: -- adrs	
LOCALS|	name1 name2 ... name-n | --	create n local values
LOOP	adrs -- L: 0 a1 a2 .. aN --	finish a loop
LSHIFT	x1 u -- x2	logical L shift u places
MAX	n1 n2 -- n3	signed maximum
MIN	n1 n2 -- n3	signed minimum
MOD	n1 n2 -- n3	signed remainder
MOVE	addr1 addr2 u --	smart move
MS	n --	wait about n milliseconds
NEGATE	x1 -- x2	two's complement
NIP	x1 x2 -- x2	per stack diagram
OR	x1 x2 -- x3	logical OR
OVER	x1 x2 -- x1 x2 x1	per stack diagram
PAGE	--	clear screen.
PICK	xu ... x1 x0 u -- xu ... x1 x0 xu	copy xu to the top of the stack.
R@	-- x R: x -- x	fetch from rtn stk
REPEAT	adrs2 adrs1 --	resolve WHILE loop
ROLL	x1 x2 x3 -- x3 x1 x2	
ROT	x1 x2 x3 -- x2 x3 x1	per stack diagram
RSHIFT	x1 u -- x2	logical R shift u places
S"	-- c-addr u	return c-addr and u describing a string.
SEARCH	c-addr1 u1 c-addr2 u2 -- c-addr3 u3 flag	search string specified by c-addr1 u1 for the string specified by c-addr2 u2.
SEE	name --	display a readable representation of the wordÕs definition.

SPACE	--	output a space
SPACES	n --	output n spaces
SWAP	x1 x2 -- x2 x1	swap top two items
THEN	adrs --	resolve forward branch
TO	x --	Typical use: x TO name
-TRAILING	c-addr u1 -- c-addr u2	u2 is equal to u1 less the number of spaces at the end of the character string at c-addr
TRUE	-- true	return true value
TUCK	x1 x2 -- x2 x1 x2	per stack diagram
TYPE	c-addr +n --	type line to term'l
U.	u --	display u unsigned
U.R	u n --	display u unsigned in n width
UNLOOP	-- R: sys1 sys2 --	drop loop parms
UNTIL	adrs --	conditional backward branch
UNUSED	-- u	bytes left in RAM
VALUE	VALUE x " name" --	Create a value with an initialiesd to x.
VARIABLE	--	define a Forth VARIABLE
WHILE	adrs1 -- adrs2 adrs1	branch for WHILE loop
WORDS	--	list all words in dictionary
XOR	x1 x2 -- x3	logical XOR

ASCII

ASCII Table 0-127 in decimal, octal, hex, binary

Dec.	Oct.	Hex	Binary	Char.	
000	000	00	0000 0000	NUL	Null Char.
001	001	01	0000 0001	SOH	Start of Header
002	002	02	0000 0010	STX	Start of Text
003	003	03	0000 0011	ETX	End of Text
004	004	04	0000 0100	EOT	End of Transmission
005	005	05	0000 0101	ENQ	Enquiry
006	006	06	0000 0110	ACK	Acknowledgment
007	007	07	0000 0111	BEL	Bell
008	010	08	0000 1000	BS	Backspace
009	011	09	0000 1001	HT	Horizontal Tab
010	012	0A	0000 1010	LF	Line Feed
011	013	0B	0000 1011	VT	Vertical Tab
012	014	0C	0000 1100	FF	Form Feed
013	015	0D	0000 1101	CR	Carriage Return
014	016	0E	0000 1110	SO	Shift Out
015	017	0F	0000 1111	SI	Shift In
016	020	10	0001 0000	DLE	Data Link Escape

Dec.	Oct.	Hex	Binary	Char.	
017	021	11	0001 0001	DC1	XON Device Control 1
018	022	12	0001 0010	DC2	Device Control 2
019	023	13	0001 0011	DC3	XOFF Device Control 3
020	024	14	0001 0100	DC4	Device Control 4
021	025	15	0001 0101	NAK	Negative Acknowledg.
022	026	16	0001 0110	SYN	Synchronous Idle
023	027	17	0001 0111	ETB	End of Trans. Block
024	030	18	0001 1000	CAN	Cancel
025	031	19	0001 1001	EM	End of Medium
026	032	1A	0001 1010	SUB	Substitute
027	033	1B	0001 1011	ESC	Escape
028	034	1C	0001 1100	FS	File Separator
029	035	1D	0001 1101	GS	Group Separator
030	036	1E	0001 1110	RS	Request to Send)
031	037	1F	0001 1111	US	Unit Separator

032	040	20	0010 0000	SP	Space
033	041	21	0010 0001	!	Exclamation Mark
034	042	22	0010 0010	"	Double Quote
035	043	23	0010 0011	#	Number Sign
036	044	24	0010 0100	$	Dollar Sign
037	045	25	0010 0101	%	Percent
038	046	26	0010 0110	&	Ampersand
039	047	27	0010 0111	'	Single Quote
040	050	28	0010 1000	(	Left opening Parenth.
041	051	29	0010 1001	)	Right closing parent.
042	052	2A	0010 1010	*	Asterisk
043	053	2B	0010 1011	+	Plus
044	054	2C	0010 1100	,	Comma
045	055	2D	0010 1101	-	Minus or dash
046	056	2E	0010 1110	.	Dot
047	057	2F	0010 1111	/	Forward Slash

048	060	30	0011 0000	0	
049	061	31	0011 0001	1	
050	062	32	0011 0010	2	
051	063	33	0011 0011	3	
052	064	34	0011 0100	4	
053	065	35	0011 0101	5	
054	066	36	0011 0110	6	
055	067	37	0011 0111	7	
056	070	38	0011 1000	8	
057	071	39	0011 1001	9	
058	072	3A	0011 1010	:	colon
059	073	3B	0011 1011	;	semi-colon
060	074	3C	0011 1100	<	less than sign
061	075	3D	0011 1101	=	equal sign
062	076	3E	0011 1110	>	greater than sign
063	077	3F	0011 1111	?	question mark

064	100	40	0100 0000	@	AT symbol
065	101	41	0100 0001	A	
066	102	42	0100 0010	B	
067	103	43	0100 0011	C	
068	104	44	0100 0100	D	
069	105	45	0100 0101	E	
070	106	46	0100 0110	F	
071	107	47	0100 0111	G	
072	110	48	0100 1000	H	
073	111	49	0100 1001	I	
074	112	4A	0100 1010	J	
075	113	4B	0100 1011	K	
076	114	4C	0100 1100	L	
077	115	4D	0100 1101	M	
078	116	4E	0100 1110	N	
079	117	4F	0100 1111	O	

080	120	50	0101 0000	P	
081	121	51	0101 0001	Q	
082	122	52	0101 0010	R	
083	123	53	0101 0011	S	
084	124	54	0101 0100	T	
085	125	55	0101 0101	U	
086	126	56	0101 0110	V	
087	127	57	0101 0111	W	
088	130	58	0101 1000	X	
089	131	59	0101 1001	Y	
090	132	5A	0101 1010	Z	
091	133	5B	0101 1011	[	left opening bracket
092	134	5C	0101 1100	\	back slash
093	135	5D	0101 1101	]	right closing bracket
094	136	5E	0101 1110	^	caret cirumflex
095	137	5F	0101 1111	_	underscore

096	140	60	0110 0000	`	
097	141	61	0110 0001	a	
098	142	62	0110 0010	b	
099	143	63	0110 0011	c	
100	144	64	0110 0100	d	
101	145	65	0110 0101	e	
102	146	66	0110 0110	f	
103	147	67	0110 0111	g	
104	150	68	0110 1000	h	
105	151	69	0110 1001	i	
106	152	6A	0110 1010	j	
107	153	6B	0110 1011	k	
108	154	6C	0110 1100	l	
109	155	6D	0110 1101	m	
110	156	6E	0110 1110	n	
111	157	6F	0110 1111	o	

112	160	70	0111 0000	p	
113	161	71	0111 0001	q	
114	162	72	0111 0010	r	
115	163	73	0111 0011	s	
116	164	74	0111 0100	t	
117	165	75	0111 0101	u	
118	166	76	0111 0110	v	
119	167	77	0111 0111	w	
120	170	78	0111 1000	x	
121	171	79	0111 1001	y	
122	172	7A	0111 1010	z	
123	173	7B	0111 1011	{	left opening brace
124	174	7C	0111 1100	|	vertical bar
125	175	7D	0111 1101	}	right closing brace
126	176	7E	0111 1110	~	tilde
127	177	7F	0111 1111	DEL	delete

SEE .S - what VFX Forth sends back

Sorry if it does not come out well formatted on your display

```
.S
( 00414808    E84F27FFFF )      CALL      00406F5C      CR
( 0041480D    E8C681FFFF )      CALL      0040C9D8      (.")
"DATA STACK"
( 00414820    E8B739FFFF )      CALL      004081DC      DEPTH
( 00414825    85DB )            TEST      EBX, EBX
( 00414827    750B )            JNZ/NE    00414834
( 00414829    8B5D00 )          MOV       EBX, [EBP]
( 0041482C    8D6D04 )          LEA       EBP, [EBP+04]
( 0041482F    E9A8000000 )      JMP       004148DC
( 00414834    85DB )            TEST      EBX, EBX
( 00414836    0F9CC2 )          SETL/NGE  DL
( 00414839    F6DA )            NEG       DL
( 0041483B    0FBED2 )          MOVSX     EDX, DL
( 0041483E    8D6DF8 )          LEA       EBP, [EBP+-08]
( 00414841    895500 )          MOV       [EBP], EDX
( 00414844    895D04 )          MOV       [EBP+04], EBX
( 00414847    BBFCFFFFFF )      MOV       EBX, FFFFFFFC
( 0041484C    E847E5FFFF )      CALL      00412D98      ?
THROW
(00414851     E80627FFFF )      CALL      00406F5C      CR
( 00414856    E87D81FFFF )      CALL      0040C9D8      (.")
"    top"
( 00414864    68D7484100 )      PUSH      004148D7
( 00414869    8BD3 )            MOV       EDX, EBX
( 0041486B    81F200000080 )    XOR       EDX, 80000000
( 00414871    F7DA )            NEG       EDX
( 00414873    52 )              PUSH      EDX
( 00414874    6A00 )            PUSH      00
( 00414876    8B5D00 )          MOV       EBX, [EBP]
( 00414879    8D6D04 )          LEA       EBP, [EBP+04]
( 0041487C    8B1424 )          MOV       EDX, [ESP]
( 0041487F    8D6DFC )          LEA       EBP, [EBP+-04]
( 00414882    895D00 )          MOV       [EBP], EBX
( 00414885    8BDA )            MOV       EBX, EDX
( 00414887    8B5C9D00 )        MOV       EBX, [EBP+EBX*4]
( 0041488B    E8CC26FFFF )      CALL      00406F5C      CR
( 00414890    8BC3 )            MOV       EAX, EBX
( 00414892    99 )              CDQ
( 00414893    8D6DF4 )          LEA       EBP, [EBP+-0C]
( 00414896    BB0F000000 )      MOV       EBX, 0000000F
( 0041489B    895500 )          MOV       [EBP], EDX
( 0041489E    894504 )          MOV       [EBP+04], EAX
( 004148A1    894508 )          MOV       [EBP+08], EAX
( 004148A4    E8EF78FFFF )      CALL      0040C198      D.R
( 004148A9    E8A672FFFF )      CALL      0040BB54      SPACE
( 004148AE    837E1810 )        CMP       [ESI+18], 10
( 004148B2    0F840A000000 )    JZ/E      004148C2
( 004148B8    E87376FFFF )      CALL      0040BF30
.LWORD
( 004148BD    E906000000 )      JMP       004148C8
( 004148C2    8B5D00 )          MOV       EBX, [EBP]
```

```
( 004148C5    8D6D04 )            LEA      EBP, [EBP+04]
( 004148C8    83042401 )          ADD      [ESP], 01
( 004148CC    8344240401 )        ADD      [ESP+04], 01
( 004148D1    71A9 )              JNO      0041487C
( 004148D3    8D64240C )          LEA      ESP, [ESP+0C]
( 004148D7    E918000000 )        JMP      004148F4
( 004148DC    E87B26FFFF )        CALL     00406F5C       CR
( 004148E1    E8F280FFFF )        CALL     0040C9D8       (.")
"empty stack"
( 004148F4    E86326FFFF )        CALL     00406F5C       CR
( 004148F9    C3 )                NEXT,
( 242 bytes, 57 instructions )
 Ok
```

MSP430 and Hardware

Until now we have looked at software only. It gets really interesting, when you start programming your own hardware, and it can run independently of the PC afterwards.

The TI MSP430 Launchpad is the probably the easiest and most inexpensive hardware to take the next step with.
Take the Launchpad, USB cable is supplied with it, write some FORTH code, Flash it onto the controller and control the chip or even some external hardware via the MSP430.

This is even getting even easier now since I started writing and extending this Tutorial.

VFX Forth LITE is now available for 2 microcontroller families:
ARM and MSP430.
Targeted at very low cost Development Kits.
The latest one I saw was from Cypress - $4.
I am sure there was a Forth person involved when they set the price.
This would be for the ARM Core.
But you can break off the USB to Serial part and interface it to a minimum MSP430 board.

The Forth here will FULLY run on the microcontroller – the PC is then used just as a Terminal. ALL of the code is stored in the MSP430 on-chip FLASH memory.

If you have Flashed your Forth program into the controller, you can run your application independently of the PC – the simplest one flashing ""SOS where is the PC"".

But this is for the next eBook, we have to start now defining the examples to be shown.

Just to show what some of the PC boards could look like – minimum versions and homemade, here MSP430 based.
The four wires are connected to the Launchpad for programming – PLUS, GROUND, SERIAL TRANSCEIVE, SERIAL RECEIVE:

… and for people who want to avoid the PCB - here a solution without: a bit of soldering and a chocolate block, and it works. Extension via screwdriver. Sticker is wrong as it has been reprogrammed with the MPE free MSP430 Lite Compiler:

No secrets, look as well at the bottom view:

I hope you enjoyed reading this tutorial and as well learnt a little bit of
Forth. The next eBook will probably be number 4 in this series, showing
Forth code examples running on this little board using the MPE Free Lite
compiler.

```
: see_you CR CR CR ." May the Forth be with you ... "
CR CR CR ;

see-you
```
Err# -13 ERR: Undefined word.
 -> see-you
\ uuuups
      ^
```
see_you
```

\\ May the Forth be with you ...

\\ ok

<u>BYE</u>

And if you have time left, have a look if there is anything of interest you can
see as part of the Forth Bookshelf.
For more advanced reading see
Programming Forth - Stephen Pelc, MPE

People

Juergen Pintaske – found the tutorial, formatted it, extended it, added all of the Forth code answers, mostly understood while testing and commenting, got permission to publish from Leo, for feedback epldfpga@aol.com

Leo Wong - wrote the chapters as skeleton for this tutorial. The starting point for Juergen.
mary.leo@gmail.com

Stephen Pelc - MPE is one of the 2 main Forth software suppliers, I used MPE's VFX to learn and make this tutorial. To contact Stephen info@mpeforth.com

Intentionally left blank for notes

Made in the USA
San Bernardino, CA
14 February 2020